Eyewitness
KNIGHT

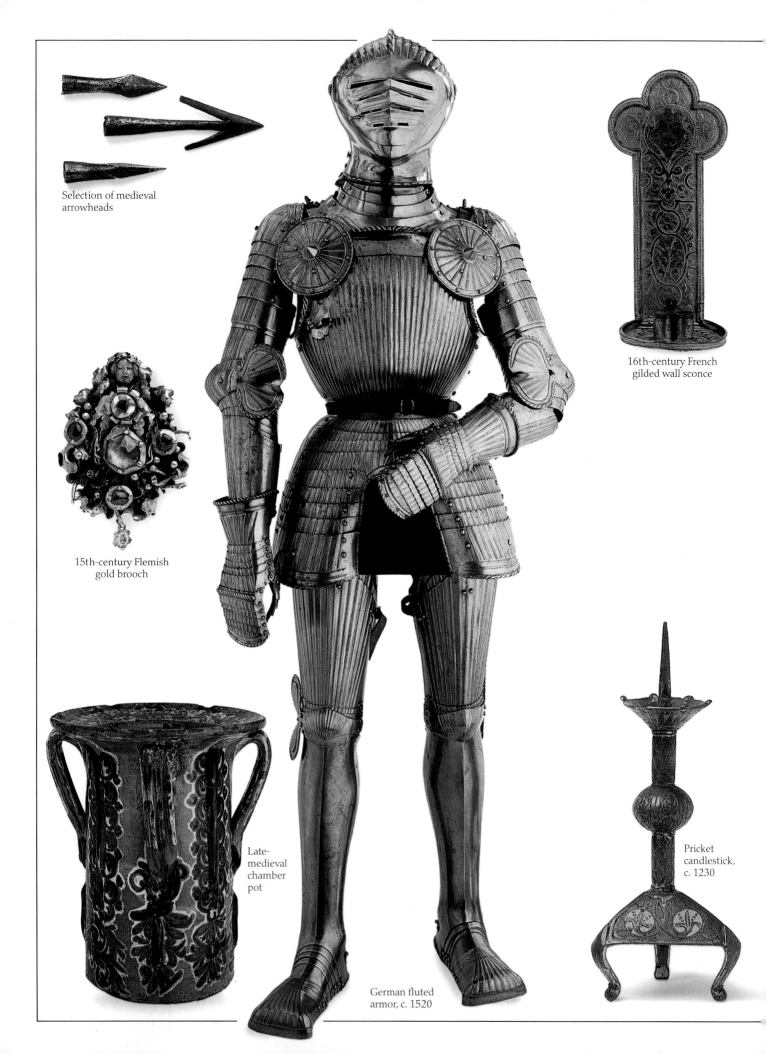

Selection of medieval
arrowheads

16th-century French
gilded wall sconce

15th-century Flemish
gold brooch

Late-
medieval
chamber
pot

Pricket
candlestick,
c. 1230

German fluted
armor, c. 1520

Eyewitness
KNIGHT

Written by
CHRISTOPHER GRAVETT

Photographed by
GEOFF DANN

15th-century
German
serving knife

16th-century Italian parade helmet

German
halberd, late
16th century

DK Publishing

15th-century spur

German
halberd,
c. 1500

DK

LONDON, NEW YORK,
MELBOURNE, MUNICH, and DELHI

Project editor Phil Wilkinson
Art editor Ann Cannings
Managing editor Helen Parker
Managing art editor Julia Harris
Production Louise Barratt
Picture research Kathy Lockley

THIS EDITION
Editor Sue Nicholson
Managing editor Camilla Hallinan
Managing art editor Martin Wilson
Publishing manager Sunita Gahir
Category publisher Andrea Pinnington
Production editors Andy Hilliard,
Laragh Kedwell, Hitesh Patel
Production controller Angela Graef
U.S. editors Margaret Parrish, John Searcy

15th-century Flemish shaffron
(armor for horse's head)

This Eyewitness ® Guide has been conceived by
Dorling Kindersley Limited and Editions Gallimard

This edition published in the United States in 2007
by DK Publishing, 375 Hudson Street, New York, NY 10014

10 11 10 9 8 7 6 5 4 3 2
KD087–04/07

Plaque from a tomb ornament
showing a knight on horseback

A catalog record for this book is
available from the Library of Congress.

ISBN 978-0-7566-3003-4 (HC)
978-0-7566-0695-4 (Library Binding)

Color reproduction by Colourscan, Singapore
Printed by Toppan Printing Co. (Shenzhen) Ltd., China

16th-
century
German
sword

Discover more at
www.dk.com

15th-century
Italian barbute

Contents

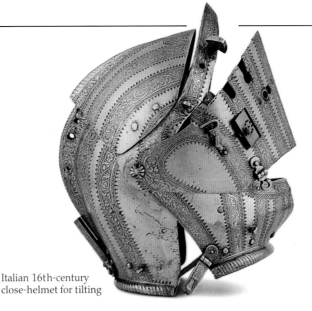

Italian 16th-century
close-helmet for tilting

The first knights

IN THE FOURTH CENTURY CE, the Roman Empire and Europe were invaded by various barbarian tribes. One of the dominant groups were the Franks of central and western Europe, who gradually expanded their power until, in 800 CE, their leader Charlemagne became Emperor of the West. Charlemagne and his ancestors had added to the number of horsemen in their army, giving land to mounted warriors. In the ninth century, this vast empire broke up into smaller pieces. Local powerful lords and their mounted warriors offered protection to peasants, who became their serfs in return. In this feudal system, which first developed in western Europe, the lords themselves owed allegiance to greater lords, and all were bound by oaths of loyalty. All these lords, and some of the men who served them, were knights—warriors who fought on horseback. By the 11th century a new social order was formed by armored knights, who served a local lord, count, or duke, and were in turn served by serfs.

WINGED SPEAR *right*
Charlemagne's infantrymen (foot soldiers) usually carried spears with lugs that stuck out, but cavalrymen (mounted warriors) may have used smaller versions as well. The lugs could keep a weapon from sliding down the shaft, or prevent the spear from getting stuck in an opponent's body. They may also have helped if the spear was used for fencing.

CAROLINGIAN CAVALRY
Under Charlemagne and his sons (the Carolingians), armored horsemen became more and more important. In this manuscript from the late ninth century, the men have coats of scale armor, helmets, shields, and spears. They now ride with stirrups for a more secure seat. The man in front carries a dragon banner shaped like a windsock.

Sharp, double-edged blade

Lug

Socket to insert shaft

BARBARIAN HORSEMAN
When the Roman Empire broke up, many horsemen from eastern Europe arrived in the west. This plaque shows a Lombard horseman of about 600. Unlike a later knight, he uses no stirrups or saddle, but horsemen like him were the forerunners of the mounted warriors of later centuries.

Double-edged blade

Iron crossguard

Tang of blade, missing its wooden grip

CUTTING EDGE
The double-edged slashing sword was the most highly prized of weapons, and the most difficult and expensive to make. At first only wealthy people, such as those with enough money for a warhorse, could afford one, so the sword became the typical weapon of the knight.

Flaring blade

KINGS AND NOBLES
The king and all his nobles were knights; there were also some knights who were not members of the nobility. In this 10th-century scene, the king sits in close conference with his nobles, the men whose armed might kept him on the throne.

BATTLE AX
The ax with a flaring blade developed in northern Europe. It was especially popular with the Viking warriors from Scandinavia, who fought on foot, but lost favor with European mounted knights. Used by well-drilled infantry, it could prove lethal to horsemen, especially when mounted on a yard-long haft (handle) and swung in both hands.

AX HEAD
Many of the tribes living in Europe after the fall of Rome fought on foot. The increase in mounted warfare was gradual. This ax head is from Germany, where feudalism and knighthood were slow in coming.

CHARGE!
Cavalrymen send their opponents flying in this Italian manuscript from 1028. All the knights wear coats of mail (pp. 12–13) with mail hoods and iron helmets. Straps around the horses' chests and hindquarters hold their saddles in place. These warriors look like tough, practical fighting men rather than the courteous knights of chivalry.

The Normans

I<small>N AN ATTEMPT</small> to stop the Vikings raiding his territory in northern France, Charles III of France gave some land to a group of these northern invaders in 911. Their new home was called Normandy (the land of the North-men), and their leader, Rollo, became its first duke. The Vikings fought on foot, but the later Normans, as they became known, copied the French use of mounted knights and became terrifying fighters. When King Edward the Confessor of England died in 1066, his cousin, Duke William of Normandy, claimed he had been promised the English throne and invaded with an army. He defeated the new king, Harold, in battle near Hastings, and brought the feudal system to England. Around the same time, Norman adventurers invaded parts of southern Italy and Sicily.

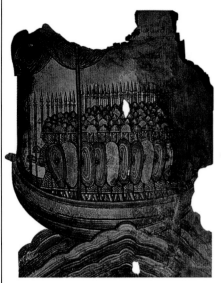

SEABORNE ARMY
Grim-faced armored soldiers with spears and wooden shields shaped like kites stand ready on the deck of a ship. This French manuscript from the 11th century shows ships like those used by the Normans to bring their invading army to England.

Metal boss

SHIELDED FROM DANGER
This little 12th-century bronze figurine shows that knightly equipment changed slowly after the Norman Conquest. The top of the helmet is tilted slightly forward, and the figure wears a long undergarment below the mailcoat, on which long sleeves were now common. The shield has a decorative metal boss (ornament) in the center.

Prick

Leather straps were originally attached here

PRICK SPUR
This 11th-century prick spur is made of tin-plated iron. It was fastened to the knight's foot by straps riveted to its arms. Spurs came to be worn by many different classes, but they were always especially associated with knights.

Arm

Position of band to attach strap

Mouthpiece

Double-edged cutting blade

RIDING TO THE ATTACK *above*
This is a scene from the Bayeux Tapestry, an embroidered tapestry probably made within 20 years of the Battle of Hastings. It shows Norman knights who wear mailcoats with hoods and iron helmets with noseguards. They carry shields shaped like kites, swords, and light lances. The small flags, called pennons, on the lances indicate that they are men of high rank.

SHIELD WALL

In this scene from the Bayeux Tapestry, the English defend their hilltop position at Hastings. Unlike the Normans, the English fought on foot. The armor and weapons of the higher-ranking troops are similar to those of the Normans, except for the large two-handed ax at the shoulder of the left-hand figure. Bundles of javelins and a flying mace can be seen. Norman arrows have stuck in their shields.

SOLID FAITH

The Normans used stone not only to build some of their castles (pp. 22–23), but also for large cathedrals, abbeys, and churches throughout their newly conquered English kingdom. They used the Romanesque style of architecture that was fashionable in Europe in the 11th and 12th centuries. Massive columns and rounded arches, seen here in the nave of Durham Cathedral, England, were typical of the style.

NOBBLER

This bronze mace may date from the 12th century and is fitted to a modern haft. The molded knobs could break an opponent's bones under his flexible chain mail.

Protrusion could pierce mail

Carving of mythical beasts

Charioteer

Wrestlers

BLOW YOUR HORN

Horns were used not only to make music and announce dinner, but also to signal on the battlefield. This one, made in the 11th century from an elephant's tusk, comes from southern Italy. The Normans settled much of this area and conquered Sicily. Because it lay on profitable trade routes across the Mediterranean, the island had a rich mixture of Byzantine and Muslim culture.

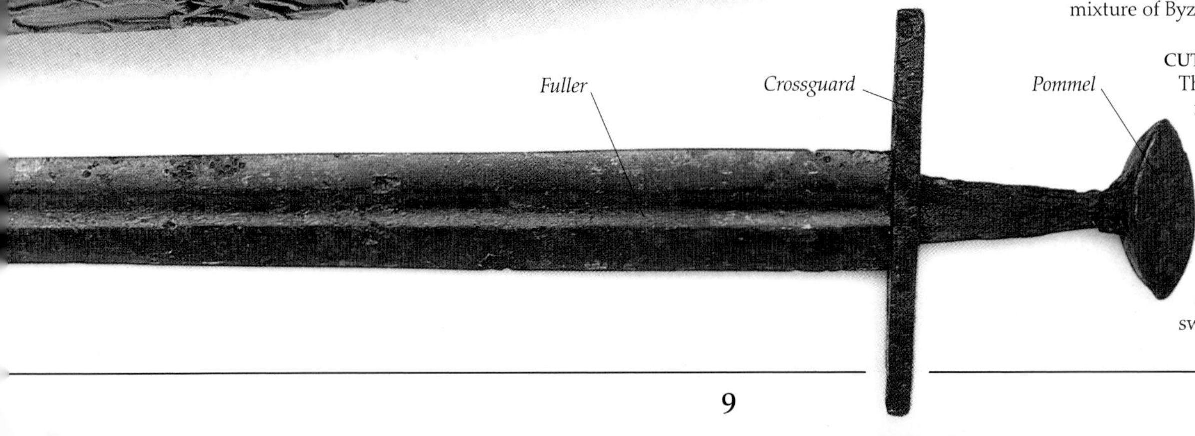

CUTTING EDGE

The sword was the knight's main weapon. This double-edged cutting sword has a groove, called a fuller, running down the blade to make it lighter. The pommel, shaped like a brazil nut, helps counter the weight of the blade and makes the sword easier to handle.

Fuller

Crossguard

Pommel

Making a knight

WHEN HE WAS ABOUT SEVEN YEARS OLD, a boy of noble birth who was going to become a knight was usually sent away to a nobleman's house, often that of his uncle or a great lord, to become a page. Here he learned how to behave and how to ride. At about the age of 14, he was apprenticed to a knight whom he served as a squire. He was taught how to handle weapons and how to look after his master's armor and horses. He even went into battle with the knight, helping him to put on his armor and assisting him if he was hurt or unhorsed. He learned how to shoot a bow and to carve meat for food. Successful squires were knighted when they were around 21 years old.

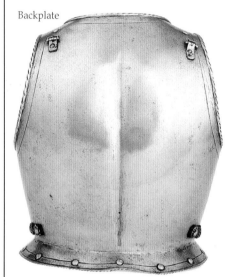

Backplate

Breastplate

BOY'S CUIRASS
These pieces of armor from about 1600 are part of a full armor specially made to fit a boy. Only rich families could afford to give their young sons such a gift.

Holes to attach tassets (thigh pieces)

THE PAGE
Sons of noble families who were sent away at a very early age to the household of a great lord or to the king's court learned a variety of skills. They were trained to serve a knight, to attend noble ladies, and to learn the art of courtly manners and good behavior.

PRACTICE MAKES PERFECT
Young men who wanted to be knights had to keep fit. So squires trained constantly to exercise their muscles and improve their skill with weapons. They practiced with each other and also sometimes with their knightly masters, who also needed to keep in shape. Training was hard and not everyone could manage it. Those who did eventually went on to become knights. This 15th-century picture shows the different ways in which the young men could train.

Putting (throwing) the stone

Throwing the javelin

Acrobatics

Fighting with sword and buckler

Fighting with quarterstaff

Wrestling

THE SQUIRE
The word squire comes from the French word *écuyer*, meaning "shield-bearer." In the 11th and 12th centuries, many squires seem to have been servants of a lower social class, but later the sons of noble families would become squires before being knighted. In the 13th century becoming a knight was so expensive that many young men tried to avoid actually being knighted and remained squires. Later the word "squire" came to mean a gentleman who owned land.

CHAUCER'S SQUIRE *above*
Geoffrey Chaucer wrote his *Canterbury Tales* around 1387. One of the stories is told by a squire, who is the lively son of a knight and about 20 years old. He could compose songs, dance, draw, and write. He was also a good rider and knew how to joust. Other stories show that some squires were not as well-mannered as Chaucer's. Sometimes they behaved like thugs. In Boston, England, in 1288, two gangs of squires, pretending to hold a squires' tournament, burned down half the town.

AT THE PEL
Squires could practice against a wooden post or pel. Sometimes they were given weapons double the weight of those used in battle; this help them get used to weapons, and developed their muscles.

AT THE TABLE
Chaucer notes how the squire carved the meat in front of his father at the dining table. Knowing how to carve properly was a skill taught to these sons of noble families as a part of their training.

DUBBING
A squire was finally made into a knight at the ceremony of dubbing. This was originally a blow to the neck with the hand; by the 13th century this was replaced with a tap with the sword. The knight's sword and spurs were fastened on, and celebrations might follow when he could show off his skills. Another knight, often the squire's master or even the king, performed the dubbing.

Thigh length leather boots

JOUSTING PRACTICE *above*
This could be done with a wooden structure called a quintain, sometimes shaped like a soldier. After striking the shield at the end of one swinging arm, the rider had to pass quickly to avoid the swinging weight.

Iron, iron, everywhere

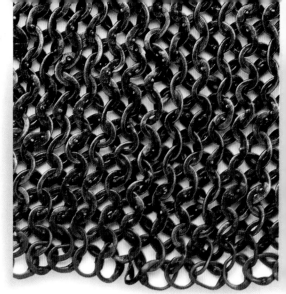

THE MAIN BODY ARMOR worn by early knights was made of mail, consisting of many small, linked iron rings. During the 12th century, knights started to wear more mail: their sleeves got longer and mail leggings became popular. A padded garment called an aketon was also worn below the mail to absorb blows. In the 14th century, knights increasingly added steel plates to protect their limbs, and the body was often even more protected with a coat-of-plates, made of pieces of iron riveted to a cloth covering. By the 15th century, some knights wore full suits of plate armor. A suit weighed about 44–55 lb (20–25 kg), and the weight was spread over the body so that a strong man could run, lie down, or mount a horse unaided in his armor. Stories of cranes being used to hoist knights into the saddle are pure fantasy. But armor did have one major drawback: the wearer quickly became very hot.

MAIL
In this piece of mail, each open ring is interlinked with four others and closed with a rivet. A mail coat weighed about 20–31 lb (9–14 kg), and most of the weight was taken on the knight's shoulders. Since mail was flexible, a heavy blow could cause broken bones or bruising.

KNIGHTLY PLAQUE
This mounted knight of the 14th century has a helm fitted with a crest. This helped to identify him in battle. However, by this time headgear like this was losing popularity in favor of the basinet and visor.

MAIL MAKER
No one knows exactly how mail was made. This 15th-century picture shows an armorer using pliers to join the links. Garments were shaped by increasing or reducing the number of links in each row, like stitches in modern knitting.

Pin allowing visor to be removed

Cord allowing mail to be removed

BASINET
This Italian basinet of the late 14th century was originally fitted with a visor that pivoted over the brow. But probably within the helmet's working life, a side-pivoting visor was fitted. The Germans called this type of helmet a *Hundsgugel* (hound's hood).

Ventilation holes

Modern mail neck guard

COURTLY GAUNTLETS
Gauntlet plates, like this late 14th-century pair from Milan, Italy, were riveted to the back of a leather glove. Smaller plates were added to protect the fingers. On these plates each cuff has a band of brass on which is written the Latin word *AMOR*, love.

SALLET

Light horsemen, who might not wear armor on their lower legs, often wore helmets like this German sallet from 1480–1510. It was originally equipped with a chin strap.

Visor with horizontal sight

THE COMING OF PLATE ARMOR

The knight on the left dates from about 1340. He wears a mail coat over his padded aketon, and over his mail coat he wears a coat-of-plates. His surcoat is short and his legs have some plate armor. The knight on the right dates from about 1420 and has full plate armor.

"Gothic style" fluted decoration

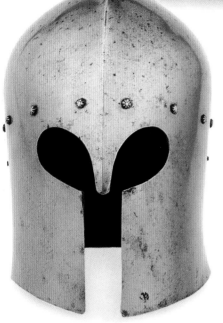

BARBUTE

Italian barbutes, like this one from about 1445, look like ancient Greek Corinthian helmets. The rosette-headed rivets secured a canvas lining band inside, to which was sewn a padded lining. Rivets lower down originally held a leather chin strap to keep the helmet from being knocked off.

UNHORSED

Fully mailed knights needed to protect themselves against heavy blows from lances or maces. This picture, drawn by Matthew Paris in the first half of the 13th century, shows the large shields they used. By 1400, thanks to the effectiveness of plate armor, shields had become much smaller.

Pointed cuff

Center plate

Articulated plates

Shaped knuckle plate

THE MAILED KNIGHT

This knight from about 1250 wears a cloth surcoat over his mail, perhaps in imitation of Muslim dress seen on crusade (pp. 54–55). His mail sleeves are extended into mittens with leather palms to give a good grip.

GAUNTLET

Typical of the long, fluted style popular for German "Gothic" armor of the later 15th century, the missing finger and thumb plates would be riveted to a glove attached inside. Plate armor like this gave better protection than mail, because it was solid and did not flex when struck by a weapon.

Fashion in steel

BY THE 15TH CENTURY, knights were protecting themselves with full suits of plate armor. The armor's smooth surface deflected the edges and points of weapons. This reduced the impact of any blows but still allowed the armor to be reasonably light. Plate armor was often made to imitate civilian fashions. Some armors were partly painted black, both to preserve the metal and as a decoration; or they could be "blued" by controlled heating of the metal. Some pieces were engraved with a pointed tool, and from the 16th century, designs were often etched into the metal with acid. Gold plating, or gilding, was sometimes used to embellish borders or bands of decoration and, in some cases, entire armors.

"Bellows" visor, so-called because of its shape

Shoulder defense made from several articulated (individually moving) plates

Besagew to guard the armpit

"Wing" on the poleyn or knee guard protected the wearer from side cuts

PUCKER SUIT
The ridges in this German armor of about 1520 imitate the pleated clothing of the time. The style is called "Maximilian" after the German emperor, even though he had no personal connection with it. It combines the rounded Italian style with the German fluted decoration of the 15th century. This form of armor remained popular until about 1530. This suit is made up of surviving pieces from several similar armors of the same period.

Blued, etched and gilded wings

Embossed, etched and gilded dolphin's mask placed over fishtailed scrolls

OPEN TO THE AIR
The burgonet was an open-faced helmet that allowed more air to reach the face than the close-helmet below. This example, with its decoration imitating the art of ancient Rome, was intended for use in parades rather than for warfare. It was made in Augsburg, Germany, in about 1520.

Burgonet

Cherubs' head

Visor pivots at the same point as the rest of the faceguard

Peg for lifting visor

PROTECTING THE FACE
A close-helmet has a visor to protect the wearer's face. This one was probably made in France in about 1575. It is covered with embossed decoration that was usually added to armor made for parades.

Figures in Roman armor

Sleeping lion

Close-helmet

14

Gorget plates attached to the buffe protect the throat

Large pauldrons made of several strips of steel joined internally by leather straps that let them move

Lance-rest helped support the weight of the lance and prevent it from being rammed through the armpit on impact

Slim plates on this falling buffe may be lowered over one another to allow more air to reach the face

Small plates on the gauntlets give complete freedom of movement to the hand

TRIUMPHAL ENTRY
This picture of King Louis XII of France entering Quenes was painted in about 1510. The colored cloth skirts popular at the time were called bases. The king's helmet is fitted with a heraldic crest.

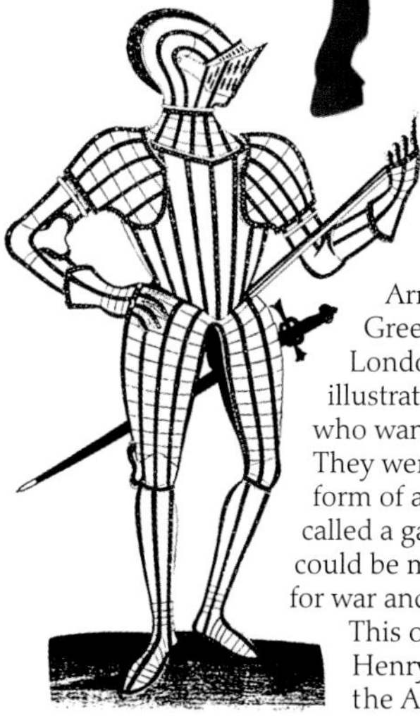

Reinforcing breast (plackart) attached to the breastplate to increase protection against firearms

MASTER DRAWING
Jacob Halder, who was Master Armorer at Greenwich, near London, produced illustrations for people who wanted armor made. They were often in the form of a set of pieces called a garniture that could be made into armors for war and tournament. This one was for Sir Henry Lee, Master of the Armories from 1578–1610.

LATEST FASHION
This armor was made for Lord Buckhurst in about 1587. It is a product of the workshops in Greenwich, near London, set up by Henry VIII. The breastplate has followed the fashion in becoming more and more pointed at the waist until, as shown here, the full shape known as a "peascod" is formed. The bulging hips allowed for thick underwear to be worn beneath. The burgonet has a triple-barred face-guard behind a removable buffe.

Poleyn has plates above and below that allow the knee to bend without exposing the hose beneath

Flexible sabaton leaves the sole exposed so the shoe beneath does not skid

ON PARADE
Three knights ride in procession, from the early 16th-century *Triumph of Maximilian*. They carry enormous parade banners representing three provinces of his Hapsburg Empire. The horses wear plate armor; the animal in the middle even has pieces to guard his upper legs—such items were very rare.

Armor, the inside story

PEOPLE OFTEN THINK that plate armor is clumsy and stiff. But if it were, it would be of little use on the battlefield. In fact, a man in armor could do just about anything a man could do when not wearing it. The secret lies in the way armorers made the plates so that they could move with each other and with the wearer. Some plates were attached to each other with a rivet that allowed the two parts to pivot (turn) at that point. Others were joined by a sliding rivet, one part of which was set not in a round hole but in a slot, so the two plates could move in and out. Internal leather connecting straps, called "leathers," also allowed this type of movement. Tube-shaped plates could have a flanged edge, or projecting rim, to fit inside the edge of another tube-shaped plate so they could twist around.

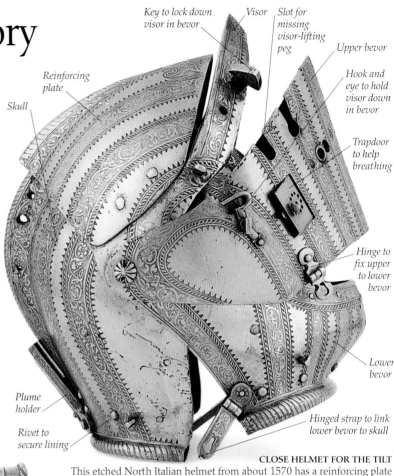

Key to lock down visor in bevor

Visor

Slot for missing visor-lifting peg

Upper bevor

Hook and eye to hold visor down in bevor

Trapdoor to help breathing

Reinforcing plate

Skull

Hinge to fix upper to lower bevor

Lower bevor

Plume holder

Rivet to secure lining

Hinged strap to link lower bevor to skull

CLOSE HELMET FOR THE TILT
This etched North Italian helmet from about 1570 has a reinforcing plate riveted to the skull or bowl. The visor fits inside the bevor that is divided into upper and lower parts. The visor and the two parts of the bevor all pivot at the same point on each side of the skull and can be locked together.

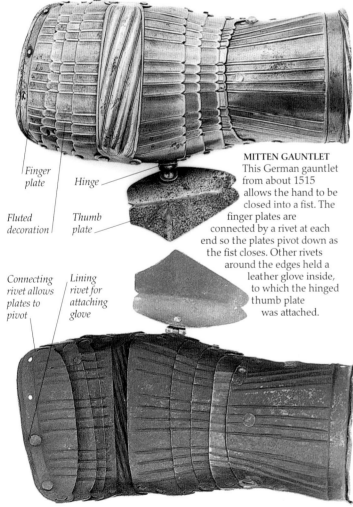

Finger plate

Hinge

Fluted decoration

Thumb plate

MITTEN GAUNTLET
This German gauntlet from about 1515 allows the hand to be closed into a fist. The finger plates are connected by a rivet at each end so the plates pivot down as the fist closes. Other rivets around the edges held a leather glove inside, to which the hinged thumb plate was attached.

Connecting rivet allows plates to pivot

Lining rivet for attaching glove

HOT WORK
An armorer has heated a piece of metal in a furnace to soften it and is hammering it into shape over an anvil set in a tree trunk. A bellows forces air over the fire to raise the temperature.

Connecting leather (replacement)

Couter

Hole for sprung stud on rear plate to close lower cannon

Hinge

Lower cannon of vambrace

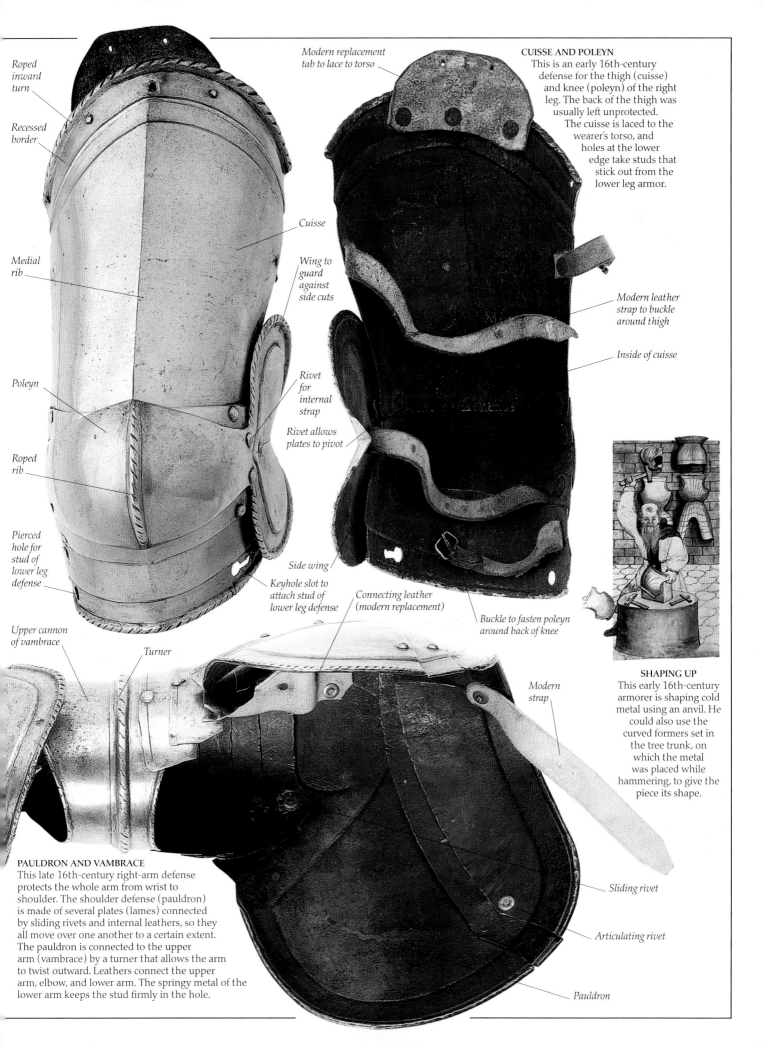

Roped inward turn

Recessed border

Medial rib

Poleyn

Roped rib

Pierced hole for stud of lower leg defense

Cuisse

Wing to guard against side cuts

Rivet for internal strap

Rivet allows plates to pivot

Side wing

Keyhole slot to attach stud of lower leg defense

Modern replacement tab to lace to torso

CUISSE AND POLEYN
This is an early 16th-century defense for the thigh (cuisse) and knee (poleyn) of the right leg. The back of the thigh was usually left unprotected. The cuisse is laced to the wearer's torso, and holes at the lower edge take studs that stick out from the lower leg armor.

Modern leather strap to buckle around thigh

Inside of cuisse

Connecting leather (modern replacement)

Buckle to fasten poleyn around back of knee

Modern strap

SHAPING UP
This early 16th-century armorer is shaping cold metal using an anvil. He could also use the curved formers set in the tree trunk, on which the metal was placed while hammering, to give the piece its shape.

Upper cannon of vambrace

Turner

PAULDRON AND VAMBRACE
This late 16th-century right-arm defense protects the whole arm from wrist to shoulder. The shoulder defense (pauldron) is made of several plates (lames) connected by sliding rivets and internal leathers, so they all move over one another to a certain extent. The pauldron is connected to the upper arm (vambrace) by a turner that allows the arm to twist outward. Leathers connect the upper arm, elbow, and lower arm. The springy metal of the lower arm keeps the stud firmly in the hole.

Sliding rivet

Articulating rivet

Pauldron

Arms and the man

THE SWORD WAS THE most important knightly weapon, a symbol of knighthood itself. Until the late 13th century the double-edged cutting sword was used in battle. But as plate armor became more common, more pointed swords became popular, because they were better for thrusting through the gaps between the plates. The mace, which could concuss an opponent, also became more popular. Before drawing his sword or using his mace, however, a mounted knight usually charged at his opponent with his lance lowered. Lances increased in length during the medieval period and, from about 1300, began to be fitted with circular vamplates to guard the hand. Other weapons, such as the short ax, could be used on horseback, while long-handled staff weapons, held in both hands, could be used on foot.

AT THE READY
The double-edged cutting sword, shown unsheathed in this 13th-century tomb effigy, could tear mail links apart and drive them into a wound.

THE COUCHED LANCE
Early 14th-century knights charge in formation with lances "couched" under their arms. To keep their line, they rode at a trot before charging as they neared the enemy.

SHINING SWORD
This sword from about 1460 has a copper gilded crossguard. Like the weapon above it, it was probably made for a rich knight.

Copper gilded crossguard

Fish-tail pommel

Horn grip

Flange

FLANGED MACE
A flanged mace has ridges sticking out from the head to concentrate the force of the blow. Maces like this may have been used as early as the 11th century but became more popular in the 14th century as more plate armor was worn. This example has a bronze head mounted on a modern haft. An iron ball attached to a haft by a chain was called a flail; this was usually used on foot.

Modern haft

Maker's mark

BLOODY BUSINESS *right*
When a dagger was used, the opponent was often grasped around the neck before the fatal blow was struck. This often meant stabbing at the face or, as shown in this late 15th-century example, cutting the throat. Like sharply pointed swords, these daggers could also pierce mail.

GREAT SWORD
Two-hand swords were large versions of the ordinary sword and were swung in both hands to deliver a powerful blow. This one, possibly made in England, dates from about 1450. Large swords began to become popular in the 13th century and a knight would often hang one from his saddle in addition to his usual sword.

Fishtail pommel

Modern cord grip

Diamond-section blade

Diamond-profile blade — *Crossguard* — *Modern cord grip* — *Wheel pommel with cap*

GETTING THE POINT
On this sharply pointed war sword of the second half of the 14th century, the old-style blade with a central groove or fuller has been replaced by a stiffer one with a diamond-shaped profile. This assisted the thrust. The point could burst apart the links of a piece of mail.

DEATH OR GLORY
The impact of two riders closing at about 60 mph (100 kph) made the pointed lance a lethal weapon. In this early 15th-century picture a knight's lance has passed his opponent's shield and punched through his armor. The figure on the left has a heavy-bladed cutting sword called a falchion. A pollax, a staff weapon to be used on foot, lies on the ground.

WEAPON OF RANK
This sword was probably made for a wealthy person. Dating from the late 15th century, it has a sunken hollow in the pommel that would have held a plaque with the owner's coat-of-arms.

Fig-shaped pommel

Hollow for small shield

CUTTING A PATH
This early 14th-century manuscript shows pointed swords but with sharp cutting edges. Surviving skeletons show that the force of a blow could cause terrible injuries and cuts to the bones.

SHORT AX
Knights sometimes wielded two-handed axes, but the smaller, single-handed variety was easier to use on horseback. This 14th-century example, mounted on a modern haft, has the remains of long iron langets that ran down the haft to stop the ax head from being cut off. The back is extended to form a beak.

Part of langet

Single-edged blade — *Remains of gilded decoration* — *Rondel*

DAGGER
Knights did not use daggers very much until the 14th century. This is a late 15th-century rondel dagger, so-called because of the protective iron disks at either end of the grip. It was the typical knightly dagger and was carried in a decorated leather sheath.

On horseback

THE HORSE was an expensive but vital item of a knight's equipment. Knights needed horses for warfare, hunting, jousting, traveling, and carrying baggage. The most expensive animal was the destrier or warhorse. This was a stallion about the size of a modern heavy hunter. Its deep chest gave it staying power but it was also nimble. Knights prized warhorses from Italy, France, and Spain—in fact the Spanish Andalusian is the closest modern breed to the warhorse. By the 13th century, knights usually had at least two warhorses, along with other horses for different tasks. The courser was a swift hunting horse, though this name was sometimes applied to the warhorse, with "destrier" used for the jousting horse. For traveling, knights often used a well-bred, easy-paced mount called a palfrey. Packhorses, called sumpter horses, were used to carry baggage.

FIT FOR A KING
An early 14th-century miniature shows the king of England on his warhorse. The richly decorated covering, or trapper, could be used to display heraldic arms and might be padded for extra protection. Some were even made of mail. Notice the "fan" crest.

GREAT HORSE
A destrier or "Great Horse" wears armor on its head, neck, and chest. The chest armor was partly covered in decorative cloth. The knight in this 15th-century picture wears long spurs and shows the straight-legged riding position. He uses double reins, one of which is highly decorated.

Etched and gilded decoration

Separately moving metal plates

"Eye" for leathers

Tread

MINIATURE GOAD
A knight wore spurs on his feet. He used them to urge on his horse. This 12th- or 13th-century prick spur is made of tin-plated iron. The two leather straps that passed over and under the foot were riveted to the ends of each spur arm.

Prick or goad

Rowel

ROWEL SPUR *right*
Spurs with a rotating spiked rowel on the end of the arm had replaced prick spurs by the early 14th century. This decorated copper gilt example dates to the second half of the 15th century.

FIRM SEAT
Iron stirrups, like this one dating from the 14th century, were worn with long straps so the knight was almost standing in them. This, along with the support of high saddle boards at front and rear, meant he had a very secure seat from which to fight.

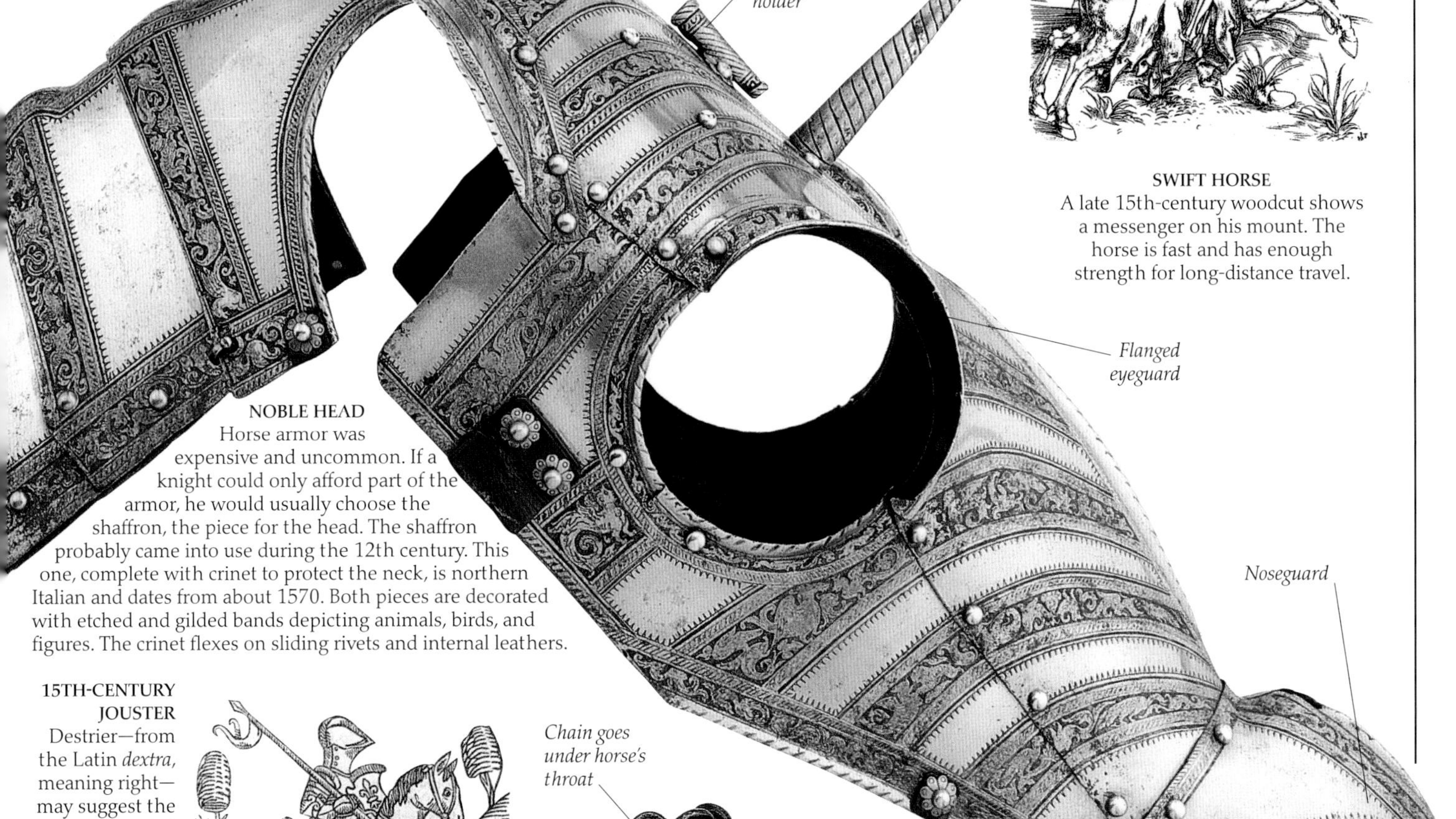

NOBLE HEAD

Horse armor was expensive and uncommon. If a knight could only afford part of the armor, he would usually choose the shaffron, the piece for the head. The shaffron probably came into use during the 12th century. This one, complete with crinet to protect the neck, is northern Italian and dates from about 1570. Both pieces are decorated with etched and gilded bands depicting animals, birds, and figures. The crinet flexes on sliding rivets and internal leathers.

Spike with spiral pattern

Brass plume-holder

SWIFT HORSE
A late 15th-century woodcut shows a messenger on his mount. The horse is fast and has enough strength for long-distance travel.

Flanged eyeguard

Noseguard

15TH-CENTURY JOUSTER

Destrier—from the Latin *dextra*, meaning right— may suggest the horse was led with the right hand, or that the horse itself led with its right leg so that if it swerved it would move away from an opponent.

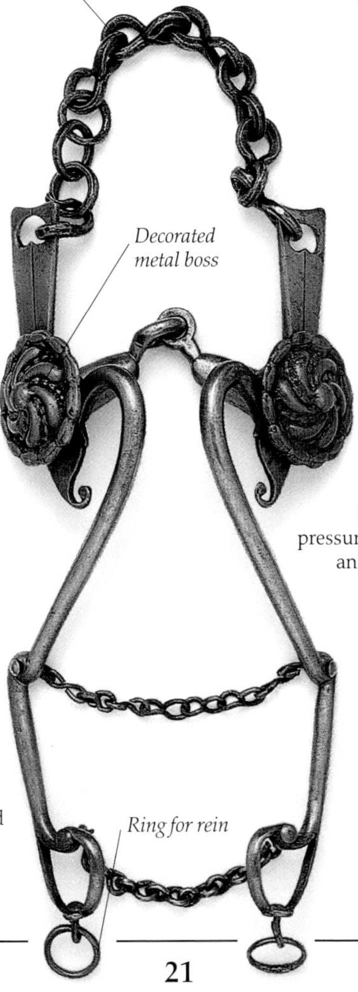

Chain goes under horse's throat

Decorated metal boss

Poll plate

FROM THE HORSE'S MOUTH
Curb bits similar to this one were used by military riders from the later Middle Ages to the 19th century. Leverage from the long arms put pressure on the horse's mouth and allowed good control.

MUZZLE
A steel frame is decorated with openwork panels and chiseled bars. At the top, a German inscription reads "As God wills, so is my aim." Below is a crowned Imperial eagle and the date 1561. Two lizards support the panel. The letters at the bottom probably indicate the owner's name.

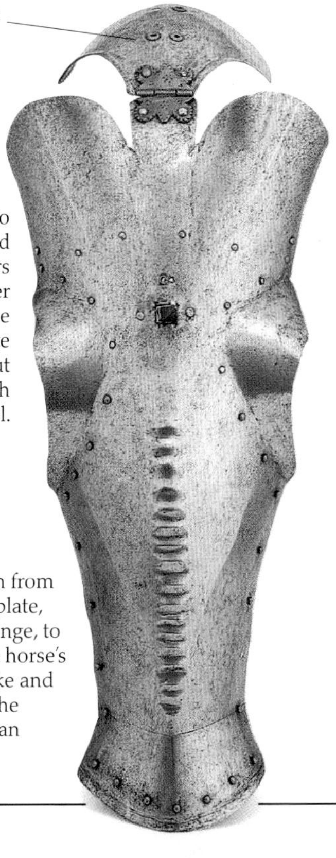

Ring for rein

SHAFFRON *right*
This German shaffron from the 1460s has a poll plate, attached by a brass hinge, to protect the top of the horse's head. The central spike and rondel are missing. The rivets originally held an internal lining.

The castle

A CASTLE COULD BE a lord's private home and his business headquarters, as well as a base for his soldiers. The first castles were probably built in northwestern France in the ninth century, because of civil wars and Viking attacks. Some early castles were built of stone, but many consisted of earthworks and wooden walls. But slowly knights began to use stone (and later brick) to build their castles, because it was stronger and more fire resistant. In the late 15th century, more settled societies, demands for comfort, and the increasing use of powerful cannon meant that castles became less important. Some of their military roles were taken over by forts that were defended gun-platforms controlled by the state.

NARROW SLIT
Windows near to the ground were very small to guard against enemy missiles, or soldiers climbing through. Such windows were narrow on the outside but sloped on the inside to let in as much light as possible.

MOTTE AND BAILEY
The castles of the 10th to 12th centuries usually consisted of a ditch and rampart with wooden fences. From the 11th century, many were also given a mound called a motte, a last line of defense with a wooden tower on top. The courtyard, or bailey, below it held all the domestic buildings.

STRENGTH IN STONE
The stone donjon, or keep, became common in the late 11th and 12th centuries. The larger ones held accommodation for the lord and his household. The bailey was by now often surrounded by stone walls with square towers. Round towers appeared in the 12th century.

MEN AT WORK
Stone castles cost a fortune to build and could take years to complete. The lord and the master mason chose a strong site and plan. Stone had to be brought in for this specific purpose. In addition, large amounts of lime, sand, and water were needed for the mortar. The materials and workforce were usually provided by the lord.

RINGS OF DEFENSE
Concentric castles, which were first built in the 13th century, had two rings of walls, one within the other. This gave two lines of defense. The inner ring was often higher to give archers a clear field of fire. Some old castles with keeps had outer rings added later that gave yet another line of defense. Sometimes rivers were used to give broad water defenses.

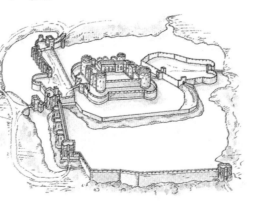

CRACKING CASTLE
Sometimes wooden fences on the motte were replaced by stone walls, forming a shell keep. Occasionally a stone tower was built on a motte, but the artificial mound was not always strong enough to take the weight. The 13th-century Clifford's Tower in York, England, has cracked as a result.

GATEHOUSE
Castle gatehouses were always strongly fortified. In Dover, England, the gate is flanked by two massive round towers. The walls are sloped at the base—the thicker masonry helps to protect them against mining. There is also a deep, dry ditch to obstruct attackers.

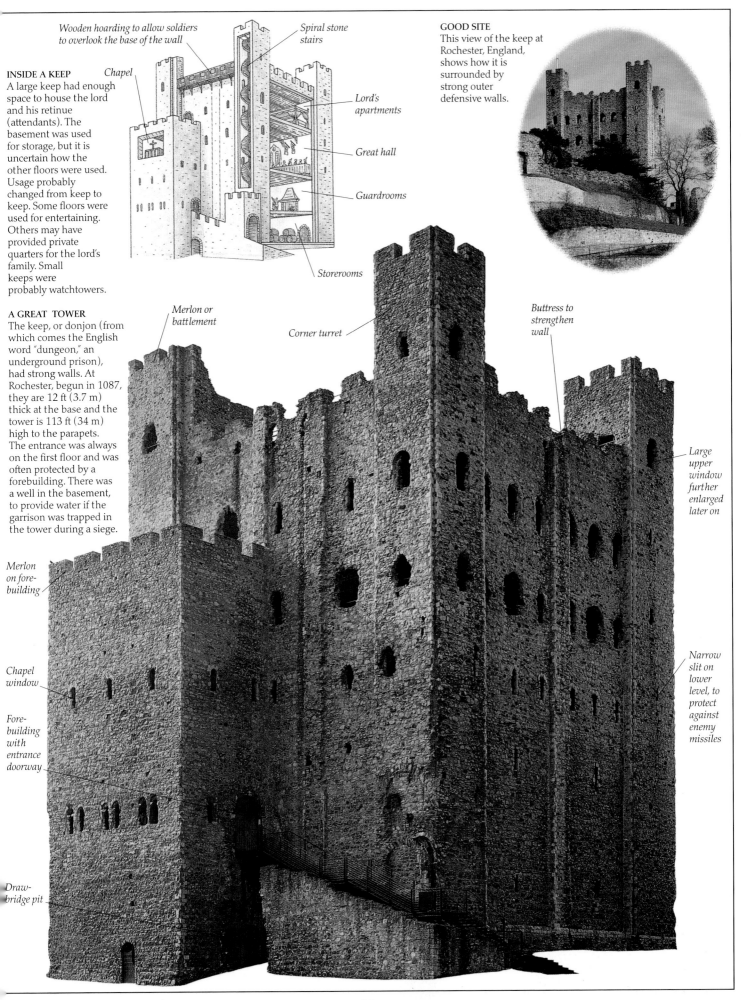

INSIDE A KEEP
A large keep had enough space to house the lord and his retinue (attendants). The basement was used for storage, but it is uncertain how the other floors were used. Usage probably changed from keep to keep. Some floors were used for entertaining. Others may have provided private quarters for the lord's family. Small keeps were probably watchtowers.

Wooden hoarding to allow soldiers to overlook the base of the wall

Chapel

Spiral stone stairs

Lord's apartments

Great hall

Guardrooms

Storerooms

GOOD SITE
This view of the keep at Rochester, England, shows how it is surrounded by strong outer defensive walls.

A GREAT TOWER
The keep, or donjon (from which comes the English word "dungeon," an underground prison), had strong walls. At Rochester, begun in 1087, they are 12 ft (3.7 m) thick at the base and the tower is 113 ft (34 m) high to the parapets. The entrance was always on the first floor and was often protected by a forebuilding. There was a well in the basement, to provide water if the garrison was trapped in the tower during a siege.

Merlon or battlement

Corner turret

Buttress to strengthen wall

Large upper window further enlarged later on

Merlon on fore-building

Chapel window

Fore-building with entrance doorway

Narrow slit on lower level, to protect against enemy missiles

Draw-bridge pit

23

The castle at war

CASTLES WERE BUILT as defenses against enemy attacks. The first obstacle for the enemy was a ditch all the way around the castle. This was sometimes filled with stakes to slow a man down and to make him an easy target. Moats—ditches that were often filled with water—were less common, but they kept attackers from burrowing under the walls. Towers jutted out from the walls so that defending archers could shoot along the walls to repel any attackers. Small gates allowed the defenders to rush out and surprise the enemy. The castle was also used as a base from which knights rode out to fight an enemy or ravage his lands.

Ironclad wooden portcullis

Wooden doors barred from behind

GATEHOUSE
The gatehouse was always strongly defended, since it was thought to be a weak spot. Usually a wooden lifting bridge spanned the ditch, and an iron gate called a portcullis could be lowered to form a barrier.

VAULTED CEILING
There are holes built into the stone vaulted ceiling of the castle gatehouse. These allowed people on the floor above to pour water down to put out fires or, possibly, to drop stones or boiling water onto the heads of attackers.

Gap (or crenel), through which defenders could shoot

Merlon to protect defenders against missiles

Round flanking tower; the shape leaves no corners for a ram or miners

High turrets gave clear views of approaching enemies

Machicolations along gate tower

Battlement on section of curtain wall

Moat

OVER THE WALLS

This early 14th-century picture shows the 11th-century crusader, Godfrey of Bouillon, attacking fortifications. His men are using scaling ladders. These were always dangerous because the defenders would try to push them away. Archers provide covering fire.

FLANKING TOWERS

This picture was taken looking up the front of the castle. Flanking towers jut out on either side to protect the gate. The battlements are thrust forward (machicolated) so that they overhang the walls. Boiling water or hot sand could be poured through the holes onto the attackers below. The holes could also be used to pour cold water to put out fires.

Stone corbel supports the battlement

EMBRASURE

An embrasure was an alcove in the thickness of the wall, with a narrow opening, or "loophole," to the outside. This allowed defenders to look and shoot out without showing themselves. In this example, the rounded lower part of the loophole is designed for guns, used more and more in warfare by the time this castle was built.

AT SIEGE
Both the attackers and the defenders of this castle are using siege engines (pp. 26–27) to hurl missiles at each other.

KNIGHTLY STRONGHOLD

Bodiam Castle in Sussex, England, was built in 1385 by Sir Edward Dalyngrigge amid fears of a French invasion. It has a single stone curtain wall with round towers at the corners, and is surrounded by a broad moat to protect the occupants. To guard against possible treachery among the defending soldiers, there are no connecting doors between their quarters and those of the lord.

Turret or watchtower

Lancet window to let in light but keep out missiles

Siege warfare

Counterpoise arm

Sling

Weighted box

AN ENEMY ATTACKING a castle would make a formal demand for the people inside to surrender. If this was rejected, they would try to take the castle by siege. There were two methods. The first was to surround the castle to prevent anyone from leaving or going in, and to starve the defenders into submission. The second was to use force. Attackers could tunnel under the wall and come up inside, or undermine the wall and bring it down. Alternatively, attackers could try to break the walls down with battering rams, catapults, or, from the 14th century on, cannons. They could also try to get over the wall using scaling ladders or a moving tower equipped with a drawbridge that could be let down on the top of the wall.

Sling pouch

Rope to pull arm down again

TREBUCHET

The trebuchet was first used in Europe in the 12th century. It worked on the principle of counterpoise—there was a pivoting wooden arm with a heavy weight at one end, and a sling containing a missile such as a stone at the other. As the weight dropped down, the sling flew up, launching the missile toward the castle. Some trebuchets had arms about 60 ft (18 m) long. On average, they could probably hurl stones of about 100–200 lb (45–90 kg) up to 980 ft (300 m).

Hauling rope

PULLING YOUR WEIGHT

The traction trebuchet worked in the same way as the counterpoise version, except that instead of a heavy weight the arm was moved by a team of men hauling on ropes. This meant that the machine was smaller than the counterpoise type and could not throw such large stones. But it could be reloaded more quickly. The sling was shorter and a man held it out as the arm began to rise—he had to remember to let go!

ASSAULT

Besiegers attack a fortress with scaling ladders while crossbowmen and handgunners cover the assault. The attackers are also using a cannon to blast holes in the stonework. More and more cannon were used in the 15th century to frighten defenders—some siege guns were enormous.

OLD AND NEW

A trebuchet towers over a gunner and his small cannon in this early 15th-century picture.

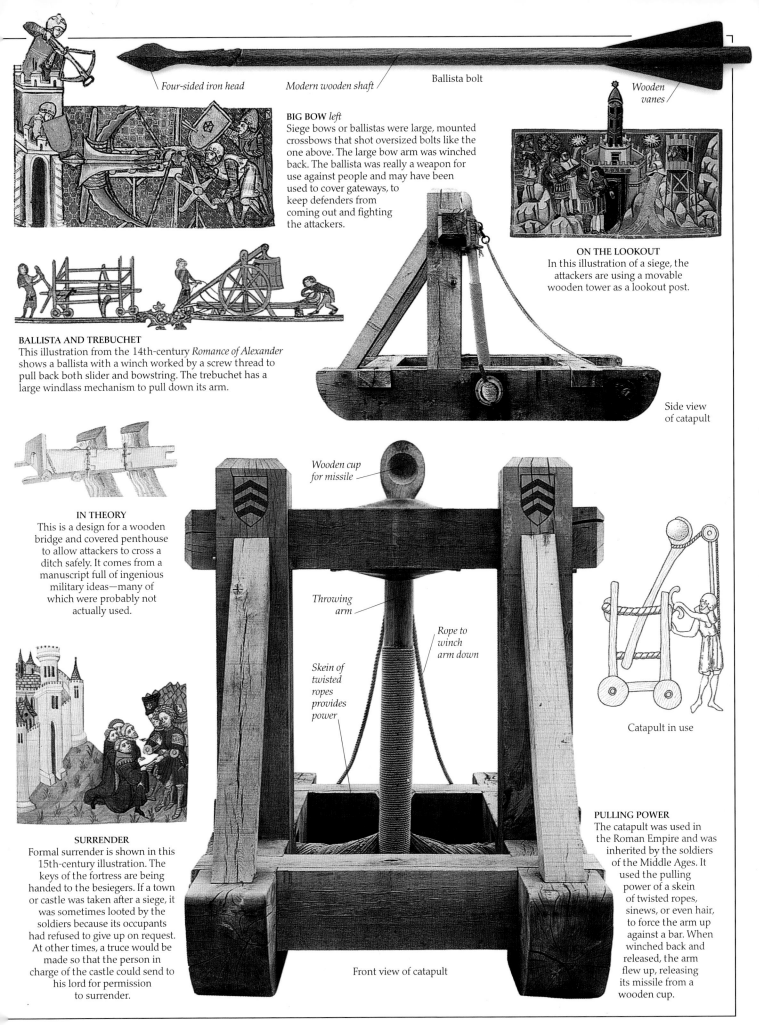

Four-sided iron head   *Modern wooden shaft*   Ballista bolt

Wooden vanes

BIG BOW *left*
Siege bows or ballistas were large, mounted crossbows that shot oversized bolts like the one above. The large bow arm was winched back. The ballista was really a weapon for use against people and may have been used to cover gateways, to keep defenders from coming out and fighting the attackers.

ON THE LOOKOUT
In this illustration of a siege, the attackers are using a movable wooden tower as a lookout post.

BALLISTA AND TREBUCHET
This illustration from the 14th-century *Romance of Alexander* shows a ballista with a winch worked by a screw thread to pull back both slider and bowstring. The trebuchet has a large windlass mechanism to pull down its arm.

Side view of catapult

Wooden cup for missile

IN THEORY
This is a design for a wooden bridge and covered penthouse to allow attackers to cross a ditch safely. It comes from a manuscript full of ingenious military ideas—many of which were probably not actually used.

Throwing arm

Rope to winch arm down

Skein of twisted ropes provides power

Catapult in use

SURRENDER
Formal surrender is shown in this 15th-century illustration. The keys of the fortress are being handed to the besiegers. If a town or castle was taken after a siege, it was sometimes looted by the soldiers because its occupants had refused to give up on request. At other times, a truce would be made so that the person in charge of the castle could send to his lord for permission to surrender.

PULLING POWER
The catapult was used in the Roman Empire and was inherited by the soldiers of the Middle Ages. It used the pulling power of a skein of twisted ropes, sinews, or even hair, to force the arm up against a bar. When winched back and released, the arm flew up, releasing its missile from a wooden cup.

Front view of catapult

Arming for the fight

Early armor was quite easy to put on. Mail was pulled on over the head, while a coat-of-plates (pp. 12–13) was buckled at the back, or sides and shoulders. Plate armor was more complicated to put on but a knight could be armed by his squire in a few minutes, and the armor could be speedily removed if necessary. After putting on a garment called an arming doublet, a knight was always armed from the feet upward, finishing with the helmet. From the 15th century, some pieces of armor were laced to the arming doublet, but in the following century these pieces were usually attached to each other by straps or rivets. Here a squire is arming a knight in late 15th-century German "Gothic" style armor.

Mail gusset

Arming doublet

Waxed points

1 ARMING DOUBLET
This padded garment has waxed thongs (called points) to fasten different parts of the armor. The armor cannot be put on without the arming doublet. The mail gussets on the doublet cover the gaps that will be left by the plates.

Cuisse

Poleyn

Greave

Sabaton

2 SABATON, GREAVE, POLEYN, AND CUISSE
The sabaton and greave, for foot and lower leg, are followed by the poleyn that is attached to the cuisse. The top edge is laced up to the torso.

Backplate

Flanged edge

3 MAIL SKIRT
Mail is secured around the waist to protect the groin, another area not fully covered by the plates. Using flexible mail here makes it easier to bend or sit.

4 BACKPLATE
The backplate is offered up into position. It has a flanged lower edge to deflect weapons from the buttocks and legs. A strap and buckle are riveted to the lower front edges.

Breast-plate

Waist strap

5 BREASTPLATE
Breast and back together are called the cuirass. They are held together by the waist straps and are also connected at the shoulders.

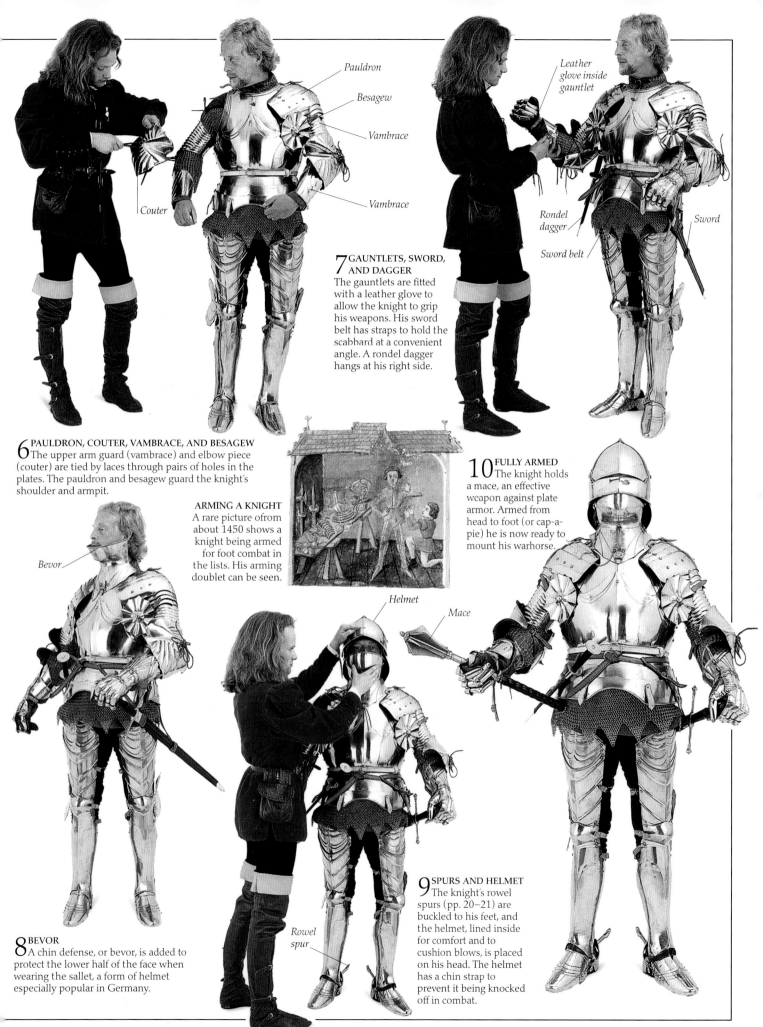

Pauldron

Besagew

Vambrace

Vambrace

Couter

7 GAUNTLETS, SWORD, AND DAGGER
The gauntlets are fitted with a leather glove to allow the knight to grip his weapons. His sword belt has straps to hold the scabbard at a convenient angle. A rondel dagger hangs at his right side.

Leather glove inside gauntlet

Rondel dagger

Sword belt

Sword

6 PAULDRON, COUTER, VAMBRACE, AND BESAGEW
The upper arm guard (vambrace) and elbow piece (couter) are tied by laces through pairs of holes in the plates. The pauldron and besagew guard the knight's shoulder and armpit.

ARMING A KNIGHT
A rare picture ofrom about 1450 shows a knight being armed for foot combat in the lists. His arming doublet can be seen.

10 FULLY ARMED
The knight holds a mace, an effective weapon against plate armor. Armed from head to foot (or cap-a-pie) he is now ready to mount his warhorse.

Bevor

Helmet

Mace

8 BEVOR
A chin defense, or bevor, is added to protect the lower half of the face when wearing the sallet, a form of helmet especially popular in Germany.

Rowel spur

9 SPURS AND HELMET
The knight's rowel spurs (pp. 20–21) are buckled to his feet, and the helmet, lined inside for comfort and to cushion blows, is placed on his head. The helmet has a chin strap to prevent it being knocked off in combat.

The enemy

KNIGHTS SOON FOUND THEMSELVES facing infantry capable of defeating them. The English axmen at Hastings in 1066 cut down Norman knights, while Flemish footsoldiers with clubs defeated French horsemen at Courtrai in 1302. Massed Scottish spear formations stopped cavalry charges at Bannockburn in 1314, a strategy also favored by the Swiss, using pikes. Different types of bow were highly effective against mounted knights. English longbowmen broke up cavalry charges by French knights at Crécy in 1346 and dismounted knights at Agincourt in 1415. The lethal crossbow shot short bolts from increasingly powerful weapons. In early 15th-century Bohemia (now part of the Czech Republic) the Hussites blasted German knights, using the first massed guns, fired from the protection of wagons.

THE LONGBOW
This type of bow was usually made of a staff of yew wood about the height of the archer himself. It usually had horn nocks at the tips to take the hemp string. War bows probably needed a pull of at least 80 lb (36 kg) and many may have been far more powerful.

Barbed arrow-head

Leather bracer

Staff of yew wood

Horn nock to take string

Arrows in front for quick reloading

SLINGER
Some lightly armed infantrymen used slings. The stone or lead bullets were lethal if they struck a man in the face, and groups of slingers could force defenders to keep their heads down during sieges. However, they could not damage armor. Sometimes a sling was attached to a wooden handle to increase range—this was called a staff sling.

A BRISTLING HEDGE
Cavalrymen were unhappy about forcing their horses against spears, and infantry in close formation with a "hedge" of spears could hold off mounted knights. It then became necessary for archers to try and break up the formations by shooting missiles. The pike was even longer and more effective.

AN ARCHER
Longbows were used in many European countries, although on the mainland the crossbow was much more popular. The English used large numbers of archers, particularly against the French during the Hundred Years War in the 14th and 15th centuries. When drawing a longbow, the string was brought back somewhere between the cheek and the ear. The leather bracer protected the arms from an accidental slap from the string; a leather tab protected the drawer's fingers. Archers wore various pieces of defensive armor, or just a simple padded doublet, as here.

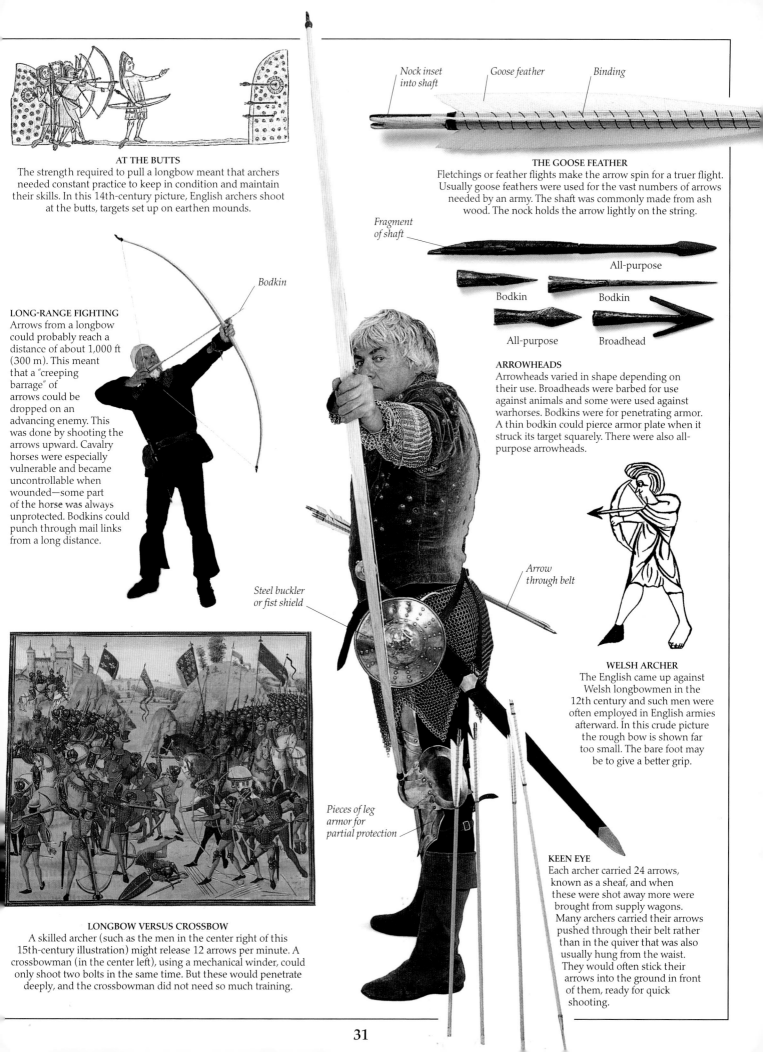

AT THE BUTTS
The strength required to pull a longbow meant that archers needed constant practice to keep in condition and maintain their skills. In this 14th-century picture, English archers shoot at the butts, targets set up on earthen mounds.

THE GOOSE FEATHER
Fletchings or feather flights make the arrow spin for a truer flight. Usually goose feathers were used for the vast numbers of arrows needed by an army. The shaft was commonly made from ash wood. The nock holds the arrow lightly on the string.

Nock inset into shaft

Goose feather

Binding

LONG-RANGE FIGHTING
Arrows from a longbow could probably reach a distance of about 1,000 ft (300 m). This meant that a "creeping barrage" of arrows could be dropped on an advancing enemy. This was done by shooting the arrows upward. Cavalry horses were especially vulnerable and became uncontrollable when wounded—some part of the horse was always unprotected. Bodkins could punch through mail links from a long distance.

Bodkin

Fragment of shaft

All-purpose

Bodkin

Bodkin

All-purpose

Broadhead

ARROWHEADS
Arrowheads varied in shape depending on their use. Broadheads were barbed for use against animals and some were used against warhorses. Bodkins were for penetrating armor. A thin bodkin could pierce armor plate when it struck its target squarely. There were also all-purpose arrowheads.

Steel buckler or fist shield

Arrow through belt

WELSH ARCHER
The English came up against Welsh longbowmen in the 12th century and such men were often employed in English armies afterward. In this crude picture the rough bow is shown far too small. The bare foot may be to give a better grip.

Pieces of leg armor for partial protection

LONGBOW VERSUS CROSSBOW
A skilled archer (such as the men in the center right of this 15th-century illustration) might release 12 arrows per minute. A crossbowman (in the center left), using a mechanical winder, could only shoot two bolts in the same time. But these would penetrate deeply, and the crossbowman did not need so much training.

KEEN EYE
Each archer carried 24 arrows, known as a sheaf, and when these were shot away more were brought from supply wagons. Many archers carried their arrows pushed through their belt rather than in the quiver that was also usually hung from the waist. They would often stick their arrows into the ground in front of them, ready for quick shooting.

Into battle

The rules of chivalry dictated that knights should show courtesy to defeated enemies. This was not just humane, it brought ransoms from high-ranking prisoners. But this code was not always observed, especially by desperate men facing death. For example, English longbowmen supported by knights slaughtered French knights at the battles of Crécy (1346), Poitiers (1356), and Agincourt (1415). And knights often showed little mercy to foot soldiers, cutting them down ruthlessly in pursuit. There was much at stake in a battle—defeat might mean the loss of an army or even a throne. So commanders preferred to ravage and raid enemy territory. This brought extra supplies as well as destroying property, and showed that the lord could not protect his people.

FIGHTING ON FOOT
Knights were trained as horsemen, but they did not always go into battle as cavalrymen. On many occasions it was thought better for a large part of an army to dismount and form a solid body, often supported by archers and groups of cavalry. In this late 14th-century illustration dismounted English and French knights and men-at-arms, many wearing visored basinets on their heads (pp. 12–13), clash on a bridge. Archers and crossbowmen assist them.

CALTROPS
These objects are only a couple of inches high, and made of iron. They were scattered over the ground before a battle to lame horses or men from the opposing army who accidentally stepped on them. Whichever way they fell, caltrops always landed with one spike pointing upward. They were also scattered in front of castles.

IN PURSUIT *above*
A mid 13th-century battle scene shows the point when one army in the battle has turned in flight and is pursued by the other side. Often the pursuers did not hesitate to strike at men with their backs turned, and once a man was down, his opponent would give him several more cuts to make sure he stayed there. Breaking ranks to chase the enemy could sometimes put the rest of your army in danger.

WALL OF HORSES *above*
Armor of the 12th century was similar in many parts of Europe, but fighting methods could vary. Instead of throwing their lances, or using them to stab overhand as sometimes happened in the 11th century, the Italian knights on this stone carving are "couching" (tucking) them under their arms. Each side charges in close formation, hoping to crush their opponents.

SHOCK OF BATTLE
This late 15th-century picture shows the crash of two opposing cavalry forces in full plate armor and the deadly effects of well-aimed lances. Those struck down in the first line, even if only slightly wounded, were likely to be trampled by the horses either of the enemy or of their own knights following behind.

One spike always points upward

Three spikes rest on the ground

SPOILS OF WAR
When an army was defeated, the victors would often capture the baggage. This could contain many valuables, especially if the losing leader was a prince. Captured towns also provided rich pickings, and prisoners and dead knights were stripped of their armor after a battle. In this 14th-century Italian picture the victors are examining the spoils.

SHOCK WAVES
This early 16th-century German woodcut shows a disciplined charge by mounted knights. Spurring their horses to a gallop as they near the enemy, the first line has made contact, while those behind follow with lances still raised. They will lower their lances before meeting their opponents.

The castle at peace

THE CASTLE DID NOT JUST house a garrison—it was home for the knight and his household. The most important building inside the castle was the great hall, where everyone had their meals, and day-to-day business was done. Sometimes there were also private rooms for the lord. There was also a kitchen (often a separate building in case of fire), a chapel, armorer's workshop, blacksmith, stables, kennels, pens for animals, and large storerooms to keep the castle well stocked. A water supply was vital, preferably a well, that could be used in times of siege. Outer walls might be whitewashed to protect them against the weather; inner walls could be plastered and brightly painted. Castles were useful resting places for nobles when they were traveling. When they were expected, the domestic apartments were made ready and the floors might be covered with fresh straw, rushes, or sweet-smelling grasses.

SONG AND DANCE
Music was welcomed as entertainment and to accompany meals. Dances usually involved many people who often held hands.

Coat-of-arms

WALL SCONCE
Only the rich could afford wax candles to burn in sconces, like this 16th-century French example. Made of gilded copper, it bears the coat-of-arms of the Castelnau-LaLoubere family, encircled by the collar of the Order of St. Michael.

AT THE LORD'S TABLE
At mealtimes the whole household would come together in the great hall. On this manuscript, from about 1316, Lancelot entertains King Arthur by telling him about his adventures.

SILVER CRUET
This silver vessel was kept in the chapel to hold the holy water or wine used in the Mass. It was made in Burgundy in the late 14th century.

Limoges enamel decoration

A GAME OF CHESS
Duke Francis of Angoulême (later king of France) plays chess with his wife Marguerite in a picture from about 1504. Being a wargame, chess was popular with knights. Chess pieces were often made of bone or ivory and beautifully carved.

BLAZING FIRE
Large fireplaces could be set in the thick stone walls of castles. The woman is spinning woolen thread (pp. 38–39).

SPIKED
This type of candlestick, called a pricket candlestick, had a long spike to hold the candle. This one, dating from about 1230, was probably used in a castle chapel.

Painted and tooled leather sheath

HAND BASIN
Pairs of basins like this, called gemellions, were used to wash peoples' hands at the table. A servant would pour water over the person's hands from one basin into the other and then dry the hands with a towel. Sometimes the water was poured from an ewer instead. This gemellion is decorated with Limoges enamels.

A knight kneels before his lady

Household musician

SERVING KNIVES
Pairs of broad-bladed knives like these 15th-century German ones were used for serving food. Each handle is mounted in brass and the grips have mahogany panels with plaques of stag horn. Each blade has an ancient swastika symbol. The leather sheath has lost its cap.

PLAY THE GAME
Board games helped to pass long evenings. Here a young man of the early 14th century plays checkers with a lady. Backgammon was also popular.

CHAMBER POT
Richer people might use chamber pots, like this one, for convenience, although castles often had toilets built into the walls. These were a seat connected to a shute that opened directly on to the outside of the castle wall.

Steelyard weight

BRONZE WEIGHTS
The late 13th-century steelyard weight was hung from a pivoting metal arm to work out the weight of an object placed on the other end. The weight on the right has the English royal arms in the version used after 1405.

Royal arms

The lord of the manor

SOME KNIGHTS were mercenary soldiers who fought only for money. Others, particularly until the 13th century, lived at their lord's expense as household troops in his castle. But some were given pieces of land by their lord. Such a man became lord of the manor and lived off its produce. He lived in a manor house, often of stone and with its own defenses. He held a large part of the manor as the home farm and "his" peasants, workers of varying status, had to work for him in return for their homes. They had to bake their bread in his oven and pay for the privilege. The lord took a portion of their goods, as did the church, although they might be invited to feasts at festivals such as Lammas (when bread made from the season's first grain was blessed). The lord sat in judgment in the manor court and might also have a house in a town for business dealings.

HOME DEFENSE
Stokesay is a fortified manor house in Shropshire, England. It consists of a hall and chamber block with a tower at each end, mostly built in the late 13th century. In the 17th century, a a wooden section was added.

Original die

MY SEAL ON IT
Noblemen often could not read or write. Instead of signing a document they used a wax seal, pressed from a metal die. This is the silver seal die, with a modern cast, of Robert FitzWalter, one of the leaders of the rebel English barons who made King John sign Magna Carta in 1215.

Modern cast

ALL IN THE GAME
This wealthy 14th-century Italian couple enjoys a board game. Knights' only other entertainment came from resident or strolling players, musicians, or poets.

Name of Robert FitzWalter, owner of the seal

IVORY CHESS PIECES
These Scandinavian chessmen, found on the Isle of Lewis, Scotland, are carved from walrus ivory and date from the mid-12th century.

Queen

King

Bishop

Knight

Warder (Rook)

UPHILL STRUGGLE
The medieval peasant had a life of hard work in the fields, growing and harvesting the crops. The 14th-century Luttrell Psalter shows peasants trying to coax a hay cart up a steep slope.

THE LORD
The status and rank of a lord varied, as did the size of his manor. Some lords were powerful men who had a number of manors, visiting them as necessary. A bailiff would look after the running of the estates when the lord was away. He might visit a town where merchants carried on their trade and where lords in need of money could borrow it from money-lenders.

GARDEN OF DELIGHT
One of the houses on this 15th-century manor is made of a framework of wood filled in with wattle and daub (mud or clay) that has been whitewashed. Close by is an orchard of fruit trees.

LIKE FATHER, LIKE SON
These details from an altar frontal from about 1500 show a knight in prayer, with his seven sons. Large families were common. The eldest son would follow his father and become a knight. Daughters would hope to marry noblemen. Younger sons and daughters often went into the church.

DECORATED CASKET
This large casket belonged to a rich family of the early 15th century. It is made of wood covered in bone panels carved with biblical scenes from the story of Susanna and the Elders.

The lady of the manor

THE LIFE OF THE LADY
The lady ruled the domestic areas—the kitchens and living quarters—of the castle or manor house. She had officials to run the household affairs, but she had to check the accounts and agree to any expenses. It was her duty to receive guests courteously and arrange for their accommodation. Ladies-in-waiting were her companions, maidservants attended her, and nurses looked after her children. The children were very important, because the lady's main role in medieval society was to provide heirs.

IN THE MIDDLE AGES women, even those of noble rank, had far fewer rights than women today. Young women were often married by the age of 14. A girl's family would arrange her marriage, and she would be given a dowry, a gift to pass on to her husband. Upon marriage, a woman's inheritance passed to her husband, so knights were often on the lookout for a rich heiress to marry. But the lady was her husband's equal in private life. She could provide great support for her husband and take responsibility for the castle when he was away. She might even have to defend the castle if it was besieged, and hold it against her enemies.

DALLIANCE
The ideal of courtly love is shown in an illustration from the medieval poem *The Romance of the Rose*. Women pass the time pleasantly, listening to a song while a fountain pours water into an ornamental stream. In reality, many women would not have had time for such activities.

THE WHITE SWAN
This gold and enameled brooch is known as the Dunstable Swan and dates from the early 15th century. The swan was used as a badge by the House of Lancaster (one of the English royal families), particularly by the Princes of Wales, heirs to the throne. Noblewomen might wear such badges to show their allegiance.

WOMEN OF ACCOMPLISHMENT
Ladies were often very well educated. Some could read and write, understand Latin, and speak foreign languages. In this picture of the 1460s, learned ladies with books represent Philosophy and the Liberal Arts.

ON BENDED KNEES
A knight from about 1200 places his hands in those of his lady in an act of homage, like that performed by a subordinate to his lord. In this case he is indicating that he will be his lady's servant—an ideal of courtly love that was not always true in reality.

BAD NEWS
A lady faints upon hearing news of her husband's death. Marriages were arranged by the couples' families, but husband and wife could and did become extremely fond of each other, and sometimes even grew to love each other.

Flemish gold brooch

JEWELS
Women liked to display their rank by wearing rings and brooches. The 15th-century gold brooch at the top is probably Flemish and has a female figure among the precious stones. The late-14th-century English brooch is decorated with coiled monsters.

English gold brooch

"SUITABLE" OCCUPATIONS
Women were expected to know how to spin wool, but some men thought teaching them to read was dangerous! In this early 15th-century picture one woman spins woolen thread while another cards, or combs out, the wool.

Pommel

Cantle

SIDESADDLE
Noblewomen were often active hunters. This medallion of 1477 shows Mary of Burgundy. She carries her hawk on her wrist and is riding sidesaddle, a method that solved the difficulty of sitting on a horse in a long dress. Her horse wears a decorative cloth trapper.

TALE ON A SADDLE
This German saddle dates from about 1440–1480. It is made of wood covered with plaques of staghorn, on which the figures of a man and a woman are carved several times. Inlaid hard wax provides the color. The figures' speech is written on scrolls. They speak of their love and the woman asks: "But if the war should end?"

Carved plaque

The ideal of chivalry

KNIGHTS were men of war, but they traditionally behaved in a courteous and civil way when dealing with their enemies. In the 12th century this kind of behavior was extended to form a knightly code of conduct, with a special emphasis on courtly manners toward women. The poems of courtly love recited by the troubadours of southern France were based on this code, and the romance stories that became popular in the 13th century showed the ways in which a warrior should behave. Churchmen liked the idea of high standards and made the knighting ceremony (pp. 10–11) a religious occasion with a church vigil and purifying bath. Books on chivalry also appeared, though in reality knights often found it difficult to live up to the ideal.

GEORGE AND THE DRAGON
According to legend, St. George was a soldier martyred by the Romans in about 350 CE. During the Middle Ages, stories appeared about how he rescued a king's daughter from a dragon. He became especially connected with England. This carved ivory shows St. George with the battlements of a castle in the background.

KNIGHT IN SHINING ARMOR
This 15th-century tournament parade shield depicts a bareheaded knight kneeling before his lady. The words on the scroll mean "You or death," and the figure of death is represented by a skeleton.

TRUE LOVE KNOTS
Medallions like this were sometimes made to commemorate special occasions, such as marriages. This one was made for the marriage of Margaret of Austria to the Duke of Savoy in 1502. The knots in the background are the badge of Savoy; they also refer to the way in which the couple's love will unite the two families.

WHAT'S IN A NAME?
This scene, from the 15th-century book *The Lovelorn Heart*, by Frenchman René of Anjou, illustrates the strange world of the medieval romance in which people can stand for objects or feelings. Here the knight, called Cueur (meaning Heart), reads an inscription while his companion, Desire, lies sleeping.

LANCELOT AND GUINEVERE

King Arthur was probably a fifth-century warrior, but the legends of the king and the Knights of the Round Table gained popularity in 13th-century Europe. They tell of Arthur's struggles against evil, and of the love between Arthur's queen, Guinevere, and Sir Lancelot that eventually led to the destruction of Arthur's court. In this story, Lancelot crosses a sword bridge to rescue Guinevere.

THE KNIGHT OF THE CART

Knights rode on horseback and it was usually thought a disgrace for a knight to travel in a cart. This picture shows an episode from the story of Sir Lancelot. Lancelot was famous for his valor and skill in combat, but his love affair with Queen Guinevere brought him shame. In this episode Lancelot meets a dwarf who offers to tell him where Guinevere is if he will ride in the cart.

ROYAL CHAMPION

Sir Edward Dymoke was the champion of Queen Elizabeth I of England. At her coronation banquet in Westminster, it was his job to ride fully armed into the hall and hurl his gauntlet to the ground to defy anyone who wished to question the queen's right to rule. Such a challenge was made at every coronation until that of George IV in 1821.

Lock

Corner reinforcement

TRAGIC LOVERS

The ivory carvings on this 12th-century box show episodes from the story of Tristan and Iseult. This is a tale of the knight Tristan, who accidentally drank a love potion and fell in love with Iseult, the bride of his uncle, King Mark.

The tournament

Fighting men have always trained for battle. Tournaments started, probably in the 11th century, as practice for war. Two teams of knights fought a mock battle, called a tourney or mêlée, over a huge area of countryside, sometimes even assisted by footsoldiers. Defeated knights had to give up their horse and armor to the victor, so a good fighter could make a fortune. At first, battle armor and sharp weapons were used, but blunted weapons were introduced in the 13th century. Other contests, such as jousts (pp. 44–45) and combat on foot (pp. 46–47), also appeared. In the *pas d'armes*, popular in the 15th century, one or more contestants held the tournament ground, or lists, and sent challenges to other knights and squires. In the 17th century, the tournament was replaced in most countries by displays of horsemanship called carousels.

"Roped" comb

BIRD MEN ON PARADE
In the early 16th century it became fashionable to wear helmets with strange, masklike visors in the parades during tournaments. Sometimes knights even wore them during the tourney itself. The visors were fitted to close-helmets (pp. 14–15). This one is like an eagle's head, with feathers etched into the metal.

Eagle's beak

Breaths for ventilation

WITH BANNERS FLYING
The colorful array of banners at a tournament was ideal for the display of coats-of-arms and all kinds of other imaginative designs. The knights also wore large crests on their helms even when these were no longer worn in battle.

Devil

DEVIL TAKE YOU
Tournaments were popular with knights, and many people liked to watch, but the church frowned on them because much blood was often spilled. In this early 14th-century picture, devils wait to seize the souls of knights killed in a tourney.

A KNIGHT DISGRACED
The women viewed the banners and crested helms of the contestants before the tourney. If a lady knew that one of the knights had done wrong, his helm was taken down and he was banned from the lists. This picture comes from the 15th-century tournament book of René of Anjou.

CLUB TOURNEY

In this type of tourney, two teams use blunt swords and clubs only. Their crested helmets are equipped with protective face grilles. Each knight has a banner-bearer, while attendants (called varlets) stand ready in case he falls. The knight of honor rides between two ropes that separate the teams; ladies and judges are in the stands. Although the lists had become smaller the artist of this picture has squashed them up to fit everything in.

Hole to take lance

Etched and gilded decoration

Face embossed in metal

Vamplate

VAMPLATE AND LOCKING-GAUNTLET

The circular vamplate was fixed over the lance to guard the knight's hand. Once the knight had gripped his sword the locking-gauntlet was locked shut so that the sword was not lost in combat. It found favor in the 16th century. Both objects are from Italian armor from about 1570.

Plume holder

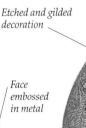

Metal plate imitating teeth

PARADE CASQUE

This Italian open helmet from about 1530 was worn in parades. It has embossed decoration and the face has been given a plate shaped like teeth. It may also have had a lower set of teeth. The hinged ear pieces are missing.

Neck guard

Locking-gauntlet

The joust

DURING THE 13TH CENTURY a dramatic new element was added to the tournament—jousts, in which knights fought one-to-one. In a joust, a knight could show his skill without other contestants getting in the way. The knights usually fought on horseback with lances, but in some contests they continued the fight with swords. Two knights would charge toward one another at top speed and try to unhorse each other with a single blow of the lance. You could also score points if you broke your lance on your opponent's shield. Sometimes they used sharp lances in combats called "jousts of war." These could kill a knight, so many jousters preferred to use a lance equipped with a blunt tip or with a coronel shaped like a small crown to spread the impact. Such combats were called "jousts of peace." Special armor was developed for jousting to increase protection. A barrier called the tilt was introduced in the 15th century to separate the knights and prevent collisions.

Eye slit

FROG-MOUTHED HELM
This 15th-century helmet for the jousts of peace was originally fastened down the back and front. The wearer could see his opponent by leaning forward during the charge. At the moment of impact he straightened up, so that the "frog-mouthed" lower lip protected his eyes from the lance head or fragments of the shaft.

GERMANIC JOUSTERS
In Germany, knights often practiced the "Rennen," a version of the jousts of war. Since no barrier was used, the knights' legs were partially protected by metal shields. The shields above their heads show that in this version of jousting they could be struck off.

Curved edge to support lance

LANCER'S SHIELD
This late 15th-century wooden shield is covered in leather. It was probably used for the Rennen. The lance could be placed in the recess in the side. The shield was attached to the breastplate with a staple nailed to the rear.

BREAKING A LANCE
Lances were made of wood and by the 16th century were often fluted to help them splinter easily. This 17th-century lance is slightly thinner than those used for jousting against an opponent. It was used to spear a small ring hanging from a bracket.

PARADE BEFORE THE TILT
Knights paraded beside the tilt, or barrier, before the jousting commenced. This scene from Froissart's *Chronicles* was painted in the late 15th century, although it depicts the jousts at St. Inglevert that took place in 1390, before the tilt was introduced. Attendants with spare lances accompany the knights.

Reinforcing bevor

Grandgaurd reinforced the wearer's left shoulder

Bolt joining grandguard to the reinforcing breastplate and to the breastplate behind

Knights took part in many different types of combat, so armors were sometimes supplied with additional pieces to allow them to be put together in various ways. The reinforcing pieces shown here are from southern Germany and date from about 1550. They are for a version of the jousts of peace known as the "tilt in the Italian fashion." Extra protection is provided mainly for the left side of the body, because the knights passed one another on that side. Knights did not need great maneuverability when jousting, so rigid extra pieces could be bolted on. These were often heavier or thicker pieces than those used on field armor. This meant that the armor was heavy and difficult to move around in, but this did not matter, because such armor did not have to be worn for long periods and safety was a priority.

Pasguard bolted to the front of the couter or elbow defense

Protruding arm to support lance

LANCE REST
This was fixed to the breastplate by staples. It helped to take the weight of the lance and stopped it from sliding back through the armpit on impact.

Large reinforcing gauntlet, here with flexible mitten-style finger plates

Strap secures a reinforcing tasset to the wearer's left side, where the greatest protection is needed

Reinforcing tasset

WATERY WARRIORS
A version of the joust was sometimes conducted on water, as this early 14th-century miniature shows. Two teams of rowers propelled their boats toward one another while a man in the prow of each tried to knock his opponent off balance.

OLD STYLE JOUSTING
These 15th-century knights are jousting in the old style, without a barrier. This style remained especially popular in Germany. The knights' lances are equipped with coronels and are placed in the shield recesses.

Foot combat

IN SOME 13TH-CENTURY JOUSTS, the knights dismounted after using their lances and fought on with swords. By the 14th century, such foot combats were popular in their own right. Each contestant was allowed a set number of blows, delivered alternately. Men-at-arms stood ready to separate them if they got too excited. From 15th-century writings, we learn that each man sometimes threw a javelin first, then the fight went on with sword, ax, or staff weapon. Later still, such combats were replaced by contests in which two teams fought across a barrier. It was called the foot tournament because, like in the mounted tourney (pp. 42–43), each man tried to break a spear against his opponent before continuing the fight with blunted swords.

AT THE READY
This detail from a 16th-century Flemish tapestry shows contestants waiting to take part in foot combat over the barrier. A page is giving one knight his helmet.

FORMAL FIGHT
Foot combats in the 15th century took place without a barrier, so the contestants protected their legs with armor. The most common helmet for these contests was the great basinet (pp. 12–13) that was outdated for war by the middle of the century.

Visor

Sword cuts

Holes for laces of cross-straps to hold the head inside

Chin piece

Hand-threaded screw

BROW REINFORCE
This plate was screwed to the visor of the close-helmet shown on the right. It gave more protection to the left side of the head.

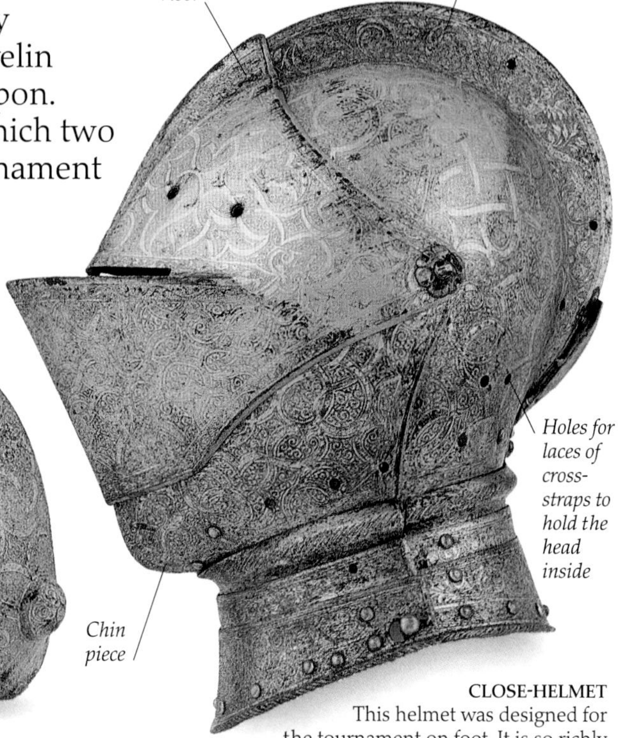

CLOSE-HELMET
This helmet was designed for the tournament on foot. It is so richly gilded that it is surprising that it was ever worn in actual combat. But the sword cuts show that it must have been used. It was part of a dazzling collection of gilded armor made in 1555.

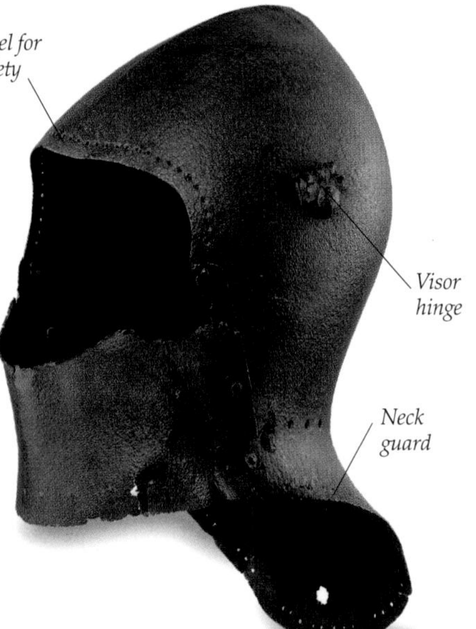

Thick steel for extra safety

Visor hinge

Neck guard

Eye slit

Lifting peg

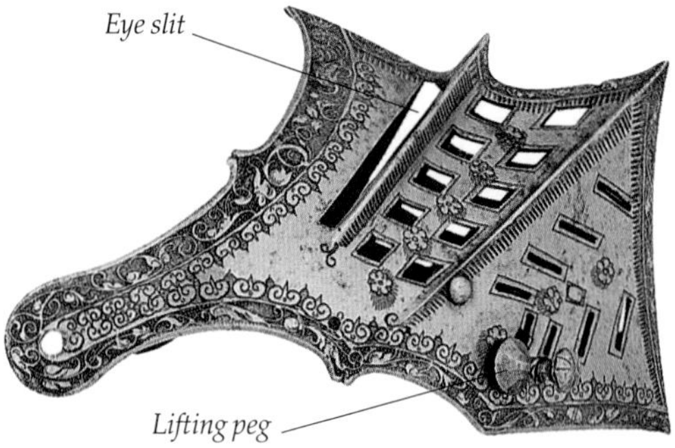

EXCHANGE VISOR
Two threaded bolts allowed the visor to be removed from the helmet on the left and replaced with this one that has a number of ventilation holes. It could be used for battle or for foot combat.

FOOT COMBAT
Helmets for foot combat and, later, the team event called the foot tournament, had to be able to withstand direct blows at close quarters, so the steel might be thicker than that on a battle helmet. This 16th-century helmet would have had a visor that locked in place with a catch. A pivoting support held up the visor when not in action.

TRIAL BY BATTLE
Not all foot contests were held for sport. Sometimes a charge of murder or treason was settled by a combat, in which God was thought to help the innocent man. The contest went on until the accused was either killed or surrendered, in which case he was executed.

POLE AX

This weapon was very popular in battle and foot combat. It was used to strike the opponent's head (the word poll means head) and the solid hammerhead at the back could concuss a man in armor. The long langets of this example from about 1470 helped to hold the head firmly and to prevent the shaft from being cut when fighting.

FOOT COMBAT ARMOR

This German armor of about 1580 forms part of a garniture, or collection, of pieces. Some larger garnitures could be made into several different armors. The surface was originally blued, and is etched and gilded with the ornament outlined in black. The visor and upper bevor lock together with a bolt. This prevents them from accidentally flying open if struck, a safety feature of some foot combat helmets. No leg armor was worn because the combat took place over a barrier and blows below this level were forbidden.

Plate to deflect side blows from the armpit

Pauldron

Langet

Rondel protects the hand

Gauntlet

THE BARRIER
This crude drawing of the late 16th-century shows knights taking part in a foot contest over the barrier.

Heraldry

Or, a pale gules

Azure, a fess embattled or

Sable, a cross engrailed or

Lozengy argent and gules

Vert, a crescent or

Azure, a fleur-de-lys or

Gules, a spur argent

M EN HAD ALWAYS decorated their shields. In the 12th century, these designs became more standardized in a system known as heraldry, enabling a knight to be identified by symbols on his shield, or a full coat-of-arms. It is often said that this was done because helmets with faceguards made knights difficult to recognize, but a more likely reason was the need to identify contestants in tournaments. Heraldry was based on strict rules. Only one coat-of-arms was carried by a knight, and this passed to his eldest son when he died. Other children used variants of their father's arms. Arms used a series of standard colors and "metals" (silver or gold) and are described in a special language, based on Old French.

BADGE OF OFFICE
This copper arm badge was worn by a servant of François de Lorraine, Hospitaller Prior of France from 1549–1563, whose arms it bears. Retainers of a lord often wore his livery badge.

COSTUME DESIGN
The fleur-de-lys, heraldic emblem of France, is used to decorate this long tunic, but true heraldry forbids gold placed on white or silver. The fur lining of the mantle was also adapted for heraldic purposes.

ROLL OF ARMS
Heralds made lists to keep a record of participants in military events like tournaments and battles. The Carlisle Roll contains 277 shields from King Edward III's retinue on his visit to Carlisle, England, in 1334.

HERALDIC JAR
Coats-of-arms were placed on all kinds of objects, to show ownership or simply to add color. This jar from about 1500 has quartered arms, in which the arms of two families joined by marriage appear twice together.

A KNIGHT'S SHIELD
This rare surviving shield from the 13th century is made from wood that has a lion rampant molded in leather. These are the arms of a landgrave (ruler) of Hesse in Germany. He is represented as a knight of the Teutonic Order, since the white shield and black cross of the Teutonic knights has been painted on the lower left.

Lion rampant

COLORFUL SPECTACLE

In this 15th-century picture, shields of the knightly passengers are hung for display over the sides of boats. Colorful heraldic banners bore the arms of their knightly owners and were a rallying point in battle, as were the longer standards that carried a lord's badges and other devices. Here the French royal arms appear on trumpet banners.

Arms of Cosimo de' Medici

SWORD ARMS

This Italian falchion, or short cutting sword, dates from the mid-16th century. It is etched with the arms of Cosimo de' Medici, Duke of Florence. It is encircled with the collar of the Order of the Golden Fleece, one of several knightly orders of chivalry.

Pommel of gilded bronze cast in shape of a lion's head

MAKING AN IMPRESSION

The bezel of this large, gold 14th-century signet ring is engraved with heraldic arms that include those of the de Grailly family. Above are the letters: "EID Gre," probably meaning: "This is the seal of Jean de Grailly." When pressed into the hot wax that was used to seal a document, the arms appeared in the wax the right way around.

Gules a lion rampant or

Or, a lion sejant regardant purpure

Gules, a swan argent

Azure, a dolphin naiant argent

Or, a dragon rampant vert

Or, a portcullis purpure

COAT-OF-ARMS

The brass of Sir Thomas Blenerhasset (died 1531) shows the heraldic arms on his coat armor, the name given to the surcoat. The version worn by this date is the tabard, also used by heralds.

SPANISH PLATE

The Spanish kingdom of Castile had a castle for its arms, while that of Leon used a lion. The two kingdoms united in 1230, and their quartered arms were first noted in 1272. On this Spanish dish, from about 1425, the true heraldic colors have been ignored, and the background has designs influenced by the Spanish Muslims.

KEY TO LABELS ON ARMS

Or	Gold
Argent	Silver
Gules	Red
Azure	Blue
Sable	Black
Vert	Green
Purpure	Purple

Azure, a Sun in splendor or

Hunting and hawking

MEDIEVAL MONARCHS AND LORDS were passionately fond of hunting and hawking. The sport provided fresh meat, as well as helping to train knights for war and allowing them to show their courage when facing dangerous animals like the wild boar. The Norman kings set aside vast areas of woodland for hunting in England, and there were severe penalties for poachers or anyone who broke the forest laws. The animals that were hunted ranged from deer and boar to birds and rabbits. Knights often hunted on horseback; this provided excitement and useful experience for war. Sometimes "beaters" drove the prey toward the huntsmen who lay in wait. Hunters might also use bows or crossbows, giving them plenty of experience with these weapons. Hawking was very popular, and good birds were prized. One 15th-century manuscript gives a list of hawks, showing how only the higher members of society could fly the best birds.

FLYING TO A LURE
A lure was a dummy bird that the falconer swung from a long cord. The falcon would pounce on the lure, so that the falconer could retrieve his bird. The lure could also be used to exercise a bird or teach it to climb high and "stoop" down on its prey.

Steel pin to engage rack for spanning bow

NOBLE BEASTS
This detail of the carving on the side of the crossbow tiller shows a stag hunt. Only rich people were allowed to hunt stags.

Wooden tiller veneered with polished stag horn carved in relief

Wooden flights

WOODEN FEATHERS
These German crossbow bolts date from about 1470. One has wooden flights instead of the feathers usually seen on arrows.

FOR DEER HUNTERS *below*
The blade of a German hunting sword from about 1540 is etched with scenes of a stag hunt. Such swords were carried when hunting and also for general protection.

WOLF HUNT
When hunting for wolves, huntsmen would hang pieces of meat in the forest and drag them along paths to leave a scent. Lookouts in trees warned of the wolf's approach, and mastiff dogs flushed it out for the hunters. This hunt is pictured in a copy of the late 14th-century hunting book of Gaston Phoebus, Count of Foix, France.

FREDERICK II THE FALCONER
This German emperor liked falconry so much that in the mid-13th century he wrote a book on the subject, from which this picture comes. Some lords even kept hawks in their private apartments.

Deer being driven into nets

Dogs chasing the deer

Hunting horn

Man shooting squirrel

Falconer

ON THE HUNT
A Flemish or German silver plaque from about 1600 shows hunting with hounds, falconry, and shooting. One hound catches a hare in front of three ladies who watch with interest from their carriage.

WEAPON AT THE READY
The crossbow was a popular hunting weapon. It could be used on horseback and easily reloaded using a goat's-foot lever or a ratchet-and-winder mechanism called a rack. The bowstring was drawn back over the nut and held there until released by the trigger, so that the crossbow could be kept drawn tight in case any game was flushed out. Crossbows for use in hunting were sometimes lavishly decorated. On this example from 1450–1470, the coat-of-arms of the owner is painted on the tiller and there are carved panels showing hunting scenes.

Original bow string of twisted cord

Revolving nut released by trigger below

Triangular barbed head

PET CARE
Hunting dogs needed a lot of care. Gaston Phoebus recommends the use of herbal medicines to cure mange, diseases of the eye, ear, and throat, and even rabies. Swollen paws damaged by thorns or spiny plants required attention. Dislocated shoulders were treated by bonesetters, and broken legs put in harnesses.

BOAR-CATCHER
The boar spear was a sturdy weapon intended to stop an onrushing boar or even a bear. To prevent the blade from going too far into the animal, a crossbar was provided. Boar sword blades were also pierced for a crossbar.

The tusks of the aggressive boar were very dangerous

AFTER THEM!
Ladies could also be avid hunters. In this illustration from about 1340 a lady blows a hunting horn as she gallops after the dogs.

Faith and pilgrimage

THE CHURCH PLAYED A MAJOR PART in the life of the Middle Ages. Western Europe was Roman Catholic until Protestantism took hold in some countries in the 16th century. Most people held strong beliefs and churches flourished, taking one-tenth of everyone's goods as a sort of tax called a tithe. Monasteries were sometimes founded by wealthy lords, partly to make up for their sins. Some lords actually became monks after a life of violence, hoping that this would make it easier for them to enter heaven. To get help from dead saints, Christians would make pilgrimages to well-known shrines, such as the tomb of St. Peter in Rome, and wear symbolic badges. Holy relics, many of them forgeries, were carried for protection.

OWNER OF THE HORN
This medallion shows Charles Duke of Burgundy who owned the Horn of St. Hubert in the late 15th century.

Container for Holy Water

WATER CARRIER
People wore tiny containers called ampullae, which held Holy Water, to protect themselves from evil. This one has a picture of St. Thomas Becket, killed at Canterbury, England in 1170, and would have been bought after a pilgrimage to his shrine.

Lead pilgrim badge of St. Catherine martyred on a wheel

KNIGHT AT PRAYER
The saints played a vital part in peoples' lives. This stained glass window from the Netherlands shows a knight from the Bernericourt family praying at a statue of Mary Magdelene.

SYMBOLS OF FAITH
People often wore badges to show that they had been on a pilgrimage. The simple lead cross shows the importance of this sign—even a knight's sword guard could be used as one. Other popular subjects were Christ and the Virgin Mary, and the saints.

Lead seal showing the Virgin Mary holding baby Jesus

SILVER CHALICE
A chalice was used to hold the consecrated wine during the Mass. This one, which was made in Spain or Italy in the early 16th century, is richly decorated, showing the wealth and importance of the church. It is decorated with six medallions that show Christ and some of the Saints, including St. James of Compostella. Pilgrims to his tomb wore badges bearing his emblem of a scallop shell.

Head of saint

HORN OF ST. HUBERT
Medieval people liked to touch or even possess relics of the dead saints, even though some had no connection with the real saint. St. Hubert was said to have seen the vision of a cross shining between a deer's antlers, and he became the patron saint of huntsmen.

Pelican in her piety

St. John

Virgin Mary

Crucified Christ

TO BE A PILGRIM
These 15th-century pilgrims are traveling to the Holy Land. Jerusalem, where Christ had been crucified and buried, was the greatest goal, but getting there meant a long and dangerous journey. Pilgrims to Jerusalem were called "palmers" and wore a palm leaf badge.

MISSIONARY
The Church was always eager to convert others to Christianity, either through peaceful teaching or by more forceful methods like those used by the Teutonic knights in Eastern Europe. Here Friar Oderic receives a blessing before he goes to the East as a missionary. Knights might also want a blessing before undertaking dangerous tasks or journeys.

St. Nicholas

THE CANTERBURY TALES
Geoffrey Chaucer (right) wrote *The Canterbury Tales* in about 1387. These concern a group of pilgrims who travel from London to the shrine of Thomas Becket in Canterbury. A knight (left) and his son, a squire, join the group, who tell stories along the way to pass the time.

Chaucer's knight

Geoffrey Chaucer

PROCESSIONAL CROSS
This early 15th-century Italian silver cross has been partly gilded and decorated with enamels. The Virgin Mary, St. John, and St. Nicholas are shown on the arms of the cross. The pelican is a symbol of piety—people thought that she wounded herself in order to feed her young, a symbol of Christ bleeding for all sinners.

The crusades

IN 1095 AT CLERMONT, FRANCE, Pope Urban II launched a military expedition to take the Christian Holy Places in Jerusalem back from the Muslim Turks who ruled the Holy Land. This expedition became known as the First Crusade. A huge army traveled thousands of miles across Europe, gathering at Constantinople (now Istanbul) before going on to capture Jerusalem in 1099. But the city was soon retaken by the Muslims and many other crusades failed to take it back, aside from a brief period in 1228–29 when the German emperor, Frederick II, made an agreement with the Muslims. Even Richard the Lionheart, the warlike English king and a leader of the Third Crusade of 1190, knew that even if he could capture the city, he would not be able to hold it. Nevertheless, western leaders set up feudal states in the Holy Land. The fall of Acre in 1291 marked the end of these states, although Christians still fought Muslims in Spain, the Mediterranean, and the Balkans. Crusades were also preached against non-Catholic heretics in Europe.

PEOPLE'S CRUSADE
In 1096, the French preacher Peter the Hermit led an undisciplined mob from Cologne in Germany toward Jerusalem. On their way they pillaged and looted, killing Jews for their money and because they believed them to be responsible for Christ's death. There were some knights in this People's Crusade, but it was wiped out in Anatolia (modern Turkey) by the Turks.

SPANISH CRUSADERS
Muslims, known as Moors, had lived in Spain since the eighth century. From the 11th century, Christian armies tried to push them back south until Granada, their last stronghold, fell to the Christians in 1492. Warrior monks, such as the Order of Santiago, seen in this 13th-century picture, helped the Christian reconquest of Spain.

Border of crowns

KING ON A TILE
Medieval churches were often decorated with patterned ceramic tiles. These examples come from Chertsey Abbey, England. They bear a portrait of Richard I, known as Richard the Lionheart, who was king of England from 1189 to 1199 and was one of the leaders of the Third Crusade of 1190.

TAKING SHIP
There were two routes from Europe to the Holy Land: the dangerous road overland or across the Mediterranean Sea. The Italian city states of Venice, Pisa, and Genoa, eager for new trade, often provided ships. Unfortunately, in 1204, Venice persuaded the leaders of the Fourth Crusade to attack the Byzantine capital of Constantinople, which never recovered.

THE MAMLUKS
The Mamluks were an elite body of troops who were slaves recruited by the Muslims. This late 13th- or early 14th-century bronze bowl shows a mounted Mamluk heavy cavalryman. He appears to be wearing a lamellar cuirass, a type of armor that was made from small iron plates laced together. Above his head he holds a slightly curved saber.

Mamluk cavalryman

Arabic inscription

A SARACEN
Many Saracens used fast horses and shot arrows at the Crusaders from their recurved composite bows. Some wore forms of plate armor, but many wore mail or padded defenses. Round shields were common and curved slashing sabers became popular in the 12th century.

TURKISH WARRIOR
This Italian dish from about 1520 shows a Turkish warrior. The crusades died out in the early 14th century and the great fortified city of Constantinople (now Istanbul) stood between Turkey and the mainland of Europe. However, the city never fully recovered from the damage it suffered during the Fourth Crusade in 1204. In 1453, it finally fell to the Sultan Suleyman the Magnificent. It has remained part of Turkey ever since.

FIGHTING FOR THE FAITH
This mid-13th-century picture shows Christians and Muslims clashing in 1218, during the Christian siege of Damietta at the mouth of the Nile in Egypt. The artist has dressed the Muslims on the right much like Christians.

STRONGHOLDS IN THE EAST
The Crusaders built stone castles and borrowed some ideas from examples in the East. Crusader castles were built on strong natural sites when possible. This huge castle, Krak des Chevaliers in Syria, was held by the Knights Hospitallers. An outer ring of walls was added in the 13th century.

CROSS-LEGGED KNIGHT
This effigy, carved in the late 13th century, was said to be that of the English knight, Sir John Holcombe, who died from his wounds during the Second Crusade (1147–49). The cross-legged pose is popularly thought to indicate a Crusader. In fact it was just a style used by the sculptors of the time.

Knights of Christ

Iɴ 1118, ᴀ ʙᴀɴᴅ ᴏғ ᴋɴɪɢʜᴛs who protected Christian pilgrims in the Holy Land were given quarters near the Jewish temple of Jerusalem. These men, known as the Knights Templar, became a religious order but differed from other monks by remaining warriors and continuing to fight the Muslims. In the same period, another order of monks, who had worked with the sick, became a military order called the Knights of St. John or Knights Hospitaller. When the Christians lost control of the Holy Land in 1291 the Templars, by now less active, found that the European rulers did not like their power and their lack of action, and withdrew their support, forcing the Templars to disband. The Hospitallers moved their base to the Mediterranean and continued fighting the Muslims. The Teutonic Knights, a German order that had become military in 1198, moved to eastern Europe and fought to convert the Slavs to Christianity.

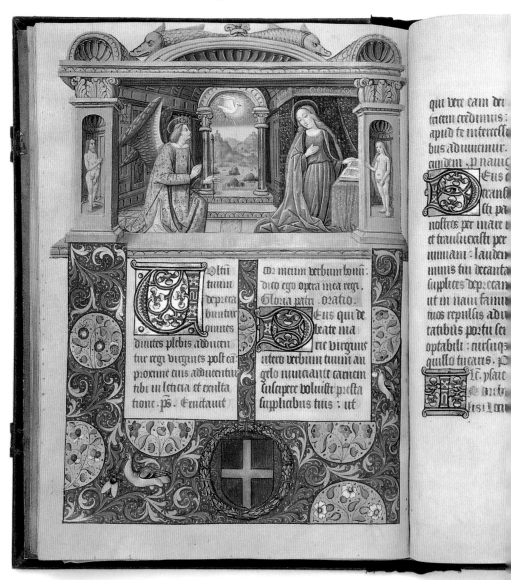

Position of original spout

MEDICINE JAR
The Hospitallers used jars made from decorated pottery called majolica to hold their medicines. Even though they were a military order, these monks had been caring for the sick since the 11th century and continued to do so, while also providing fighting men for the Christian wars against the Muslims.

THE HOSPITAL
Malta was the final home of the Knights of St. John. This engraving of 1586 shows them at work on the Great Ward of their hospital in the Maltese capital, Valetta.

BRONZE MORTAR
Ingredients for Hospitaller medicines were ground by a pestle in this mortar dating from the 12th or 13th century.

BURNING THE TEMPLARS

After the Christians took control of the Holy Land, the Templars became very rich and powerful. This made them unpopular. King Philip IV of France decided to seize their wealth. The Grand Master, Jacques de Morlay, was burned in 1313, and the Order was suppressed in Europe.

GRAND MASTER'S SEAL

A Grand Master led each military order. This seal belonged to Raymond de Berenger, who ran the Hospitallers from 1363–1374.

THE FIGHT GOES ON

After the loss of the Holy Land in 1291, the Hospitallers moved first to Cyprus, then in 1310 to Rhodes where they again clashed with the Muslims. This continual struggle meant that, despite their wealth, they managed to escape the fate of the Templars.

PROCESSIONAL CROSS

This early 16th-century cross is made of oak covered with silver plate. The figure of Christ is older. The Evangelists are pictured on the arms of the cross. The cross belonged to the Hospitallers and the coat-of-arms is that of Pierre Decluys, Grand Prior of France from 1522–1535. Each military order had priories or commanderies in several countries that raised money and recruits.

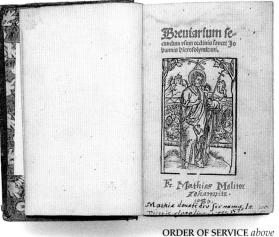

ORDER OF SERVICE *above*

The Knights of St. John were expected to attend church services and to know their Bible in the same way as other monks. Breviaries like this one contained the daily service. The religious knights had to obey strict rules that were usually based on those of the regular monastic orders. Hospitallers followed the rule of St. Benedict, the Templars that of the Cistercian Order.

KNIGHT TEMPLAR

Templars wore a white surcoat with a red cross. This 12th-century fresco from the Templar church at Cressac in France shows a knight galloping into battle.

THE RHODES MISSAL

Joining the Knights Hospitaller meant being a skilled fighting man yet rejecting the world for a monastic life. Like other monks, the knights swore to serve the order faithfully, to remain chaste, and to help those in need. It is thought that many knights took their vows on this book, the late 15th-century Rhodes Missal.

WATER BOTTLE

A water supply was vital in the heat of the Mediterranean and along pilgrim routes in the Holy Land. This metal water bottle from about 1500 bears the cross of the Order of St. John.

Knights of the Rising Sun

EUROPE WAS NOT the only area to have a warrior class. Japan developed a society similar to the feudal system of medieval Europe, and the equivalent of the knight was the samurai. Like his western equivalent, he was a warrior, often fighting on horseback, serving a lord, and served by others in turn. After the Gempei War of 1180–1185, Japan was ruled by an emperor, but the real power lay with the military leader or Shogun. However, civil wars had weakened the Shogun's power by 1550, and Japan was divided into kingdoms ruled by *daimyo* or barons. In 1543, Portuguese merchants brought the first guns to Japan: soon large, professional armies appeared. A strong shogunate was revived after a victory in 1600, and the last great samurai battle was fought in 1615.

HELMET AND FACE GUARD
Helmets like this 17th-century example are often fitted with mustaches. They have a neckguard made of iron plates coated with lacquer (a type of varnish) and laced together with silk. Lacquer was used to protect metal from moisture in the humid climate of Japan.

SWORDSMAN
Samurai prized their swords greatly. This 19th-century print shows a samurai holding his long sword unsheathed. His smaller sword is thrust through his belt, with the cutting edge uppermost so that he could deliver a blow straight from the scabbard.

FIGHTING SAMURAI
These two samurai are fighting on foot. From the 14th century on, there was an increase in this type of combat, although samurai still fought on horseback when necessary. The shift toward foot combat with sword and curved spear brought changes in the armor.

EARLY ARMOR *above*
This 19th-century copy of a 12th-century armor is in the great armor, or *O-yoroi*, style. An iron strip is attached to the top of the breast, and the rest of the cuirass is made of small lacquered iron plates laced together with silk and leather. The 12th-century samurai who wore armor like this were basically mounted archers.

Tempered edge

PAIR OF SWORDS
The main samurai sword was the *katana*, sheathed in a wooden scabbard (*saya*). The guard for the hilt was formed by a decorated oval metal plate (*tsuba*). The grip (*tsuka*) was covered in rough sharkskin, to prevent the hand from slipping, and bound with silk braid. A pommel cap (*kashira*) fit over the end. The pair of swords (*daisho*) was completed by a shorter sword (*wakizashi*) that was also stuck through the belt.

MASTER AND SERVANT
A small lacquered case, or *inro*, is decorated with a picture of a servant kneeling before a samurai. Warriors needed servants to attend them and look after their equipment—just like western knights. A samurai held life-and-death power over his servants and over the farmers who worked on his land and provided him with food.

MODERN ARMOR
From the 16th century on, Japanese armor was more solid to give more protection from bullets. This example is a 19th-century armor called a *tosei gusoku*. A cuirass, or *do*, protects the chest, each arm has a defense (*kote*) and shoulder guard (*sode*), and each leg has armor for the lower thigh (*haidate*) and shin (*suneate*). The helmet (*kabuto*) has a face defense (*mempo*) and sports a buffalo horn crest.

THE ART OF SWORDSMANSHIP
In this section from a 19th-century picture by Kunisada, a samurai called Minamoto Yoshitsune is instructed in swordplay by creatures called *tengi*. Learning to use the sword correctly took many years of hard work—there were many moves that the swordsman had to perfect. Japanese swords had extremely sharp cutting edges.

Sharkskin grip

WARRIOR
This 19th-century photograph shows a samurai dressed in his armor. This is made of solid plates of iron, unlike the earlier small laced plates. Over his armor he wears a surcoat, or *jinbaori*. He carries not only his swords, but also a long bow made of bamboo and other woods glued together and bound with rattan. His helmet crest bears a pair of horns.

The professionals

IN THE HEAT OF BATTLE, even heavily armed squadrons of knights could not break the disciplined ranks of infantry. The wars between France and Burgundy in 1476–1477 showed how mounted knights were unable to defeat solid bodies of pikemen backed up by soldiers using handguns. So by 1500 the infantry was becoming the most important part of any army. In Germany, foot soldiers called *Landsknechte* copied their Swiss neighbors by using pikes and guns. The way men were hired was also changing. Feudal forces, who fought in return for their land, were increasingly being replaced by paid permanent forces of well-trained soldiers, backed up by mercenaries and locally recruited men. Mounted knights were becoming less effective on the battlefield.

Grip covered in wood and leather

Crossguard

Lug

Ricasso with leather covering

Flamboyant or wavy edge

PUFFED AND SLASHED ARMOR
In the late 15th and early 16th centuries, the Swiss and German *Landsknechte* enjoyed showing off by wearing extravagant clothing in the "puffed and slashed" style. This German armor made in about 1520 mimics that style. The slashings are etched and gilded, while the surfaces in between are etched to suggest damask or cut velvet cloth.

Bellows visor

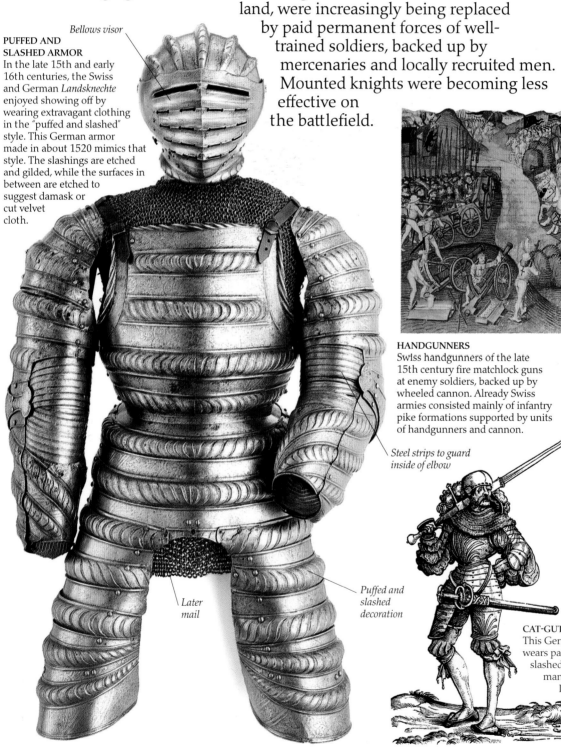

Later mail

Puffed and slashed decoration

HANDGUNNERS
Swiss handgunners of the late 15th century fire matchlock guns at enemy soldiers, backed up by wheeled cannon. Already Swiss armies consisted mainly of infantry pike formations supported by units of handgunners and cannon.

Steel strips to guard inside of elbow

TWO-HANDED SWORD
Swords like this were useful for cutting the points off pikes carried by enemy soldiers. The lugs on the blade helped to prevent an enemy weapon from sliding up to the hands. The leather covering the ricasso, or blunted section on the blade, allowed for a shorter grip on the weapon. This example dates from about 1600, by which time these were becoming largely ceremonial weapons.

CAT-GUTTER
This German *Landsknecht* of about 1520 wears partial armor with puffed and slashed breeches and a "bishop's mantle" of mail to guard his neck. In addition to a two-handed sword, he carries a distinctive short sword that was called a *Katzbalger* (Cat-gutter).

IN BLACK AND WHITE
Infantrymen who could afford some protection often chose a half armor without leg pieces to make walking easier. Light horsemen wore similar armor. The open helmet, called a burgonet, allowed more air to get to the face. The black and white effect on this armor from about 1550 was made by leaving some areas as bright steel while painting other parts black. The paint was also thought to protect against rust.

HALBERD
The heavy ax head on this infantry staff weapon could be used to maim an enemy, while the beak on the back could trip up horses or hook a knight from the saddle. This German example dates from about 1500.

Cheek piece of burgonet

HALBERDIER
This *Landsknecht* of the 16th century wears the usual elaborate costume and armor, this time surmounted by a plume. In addition to his sword, he carries a halberd, similar to the one shown on the right.

Gauntlet

GERMAN CROSSBOW
This crossbow from about 1520 has a bow made from cane and whalebone covered with parchment. When the short crossbow bolt struck armor squarely it could punch through it. Unlike longbows, which needed constant practice, crossbows were spanned mechanically (pp. 50–51) and could be used more easily. They were popular on the European mainland.

Steel stirrup

Cord and braided leather binding

Tasset

Bowstring of twisted cord

GUN BATTERY
In this woodcut from about 1520, a gunner lowers a glowing linstock to the touchhole of a cannon. The barrels have molded decoration. The increasing use of cannon was one factor in the decline of the castle and the rise of the heavily gunned fortress. Field guns were used against enemy cavalry and infantry.

The decline of chivalry

PROCESSIONAL PARTIZAN
With firearms taking over the battlefield, many edged weapons were made for ceremonial use only, like this German partizan from about 1690.

RULERS INCREASINGLY PREFERRED to use professional soldiers, leaving knights to live on their estates. By the 17th century, warfare was becoming more and more the job of full-time soldiers and mercenaries. Knights occasionally fought as officers, usually of cavalry, but the medieval fighting man was now only a memory. No longer was knighthood only granted to sons of knights. It was becoming an honor, a title given to people that the monarch thought deserved recognition. This idea still continues in many places, but the knight of old was not forgotten. His image survived, helped by old castles and stories of heroes such as King Arthur, and the magic, woven by medieval poets and 19th-century romantics, lives on.

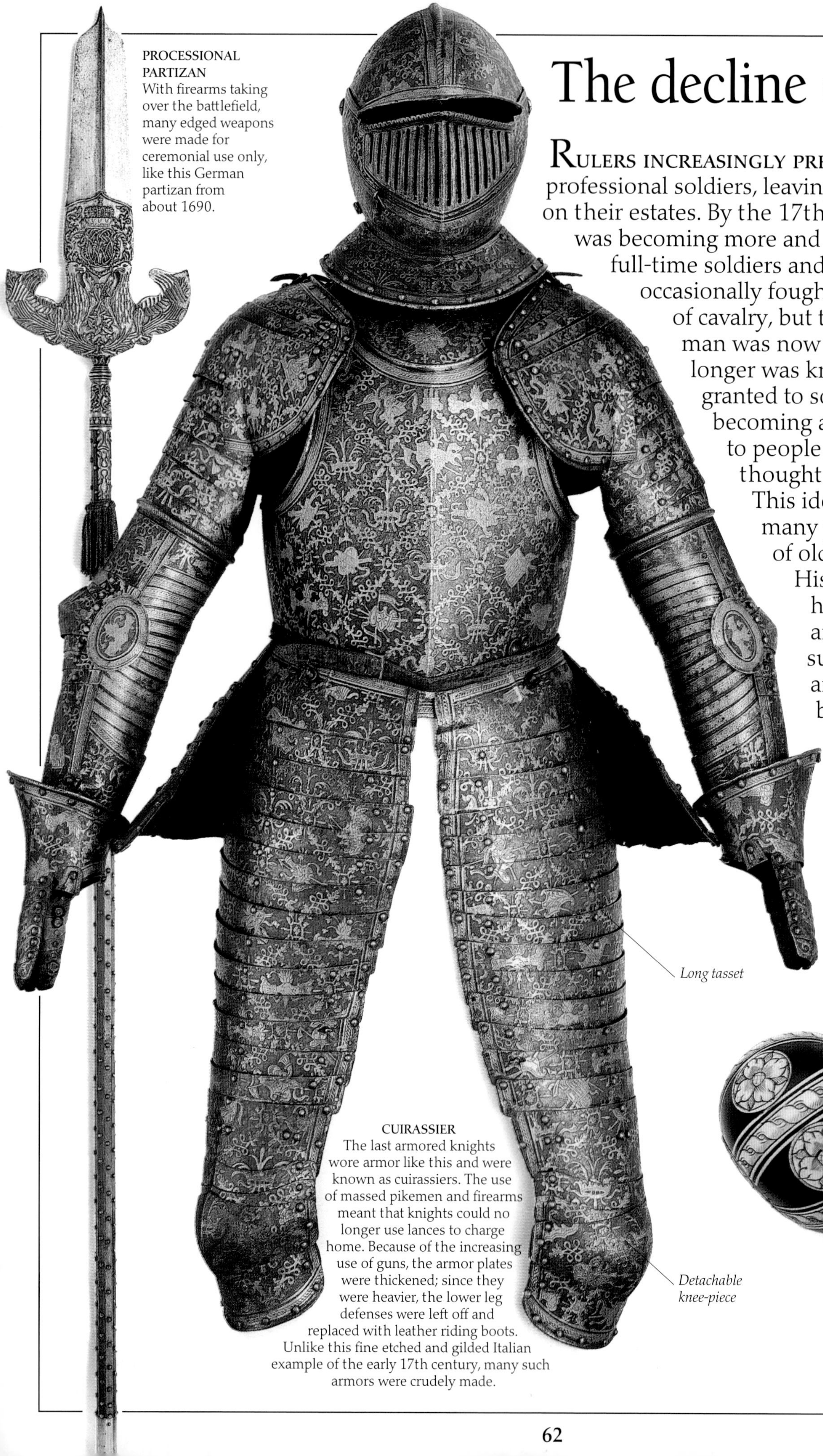

Long tasset
Detachable knee-piece

CUIRASSIER
The last armored knights wore armor like this and were known as cuirassiers. The use of massed pikemen and firearms meant that knights could no longer use lances to charge home. Because of the increasing use of guns, the armor plates were thickened; since they were heavier, the lower leg defenses were left off and replaced with leather riding boots. Unlike this fine etched and gilded Italian example of the early 17th century, many such armors were crudely made.

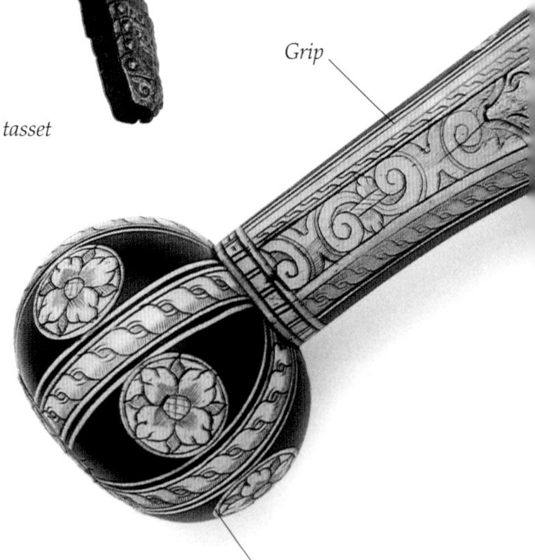

Grip
Butt could be used as a club

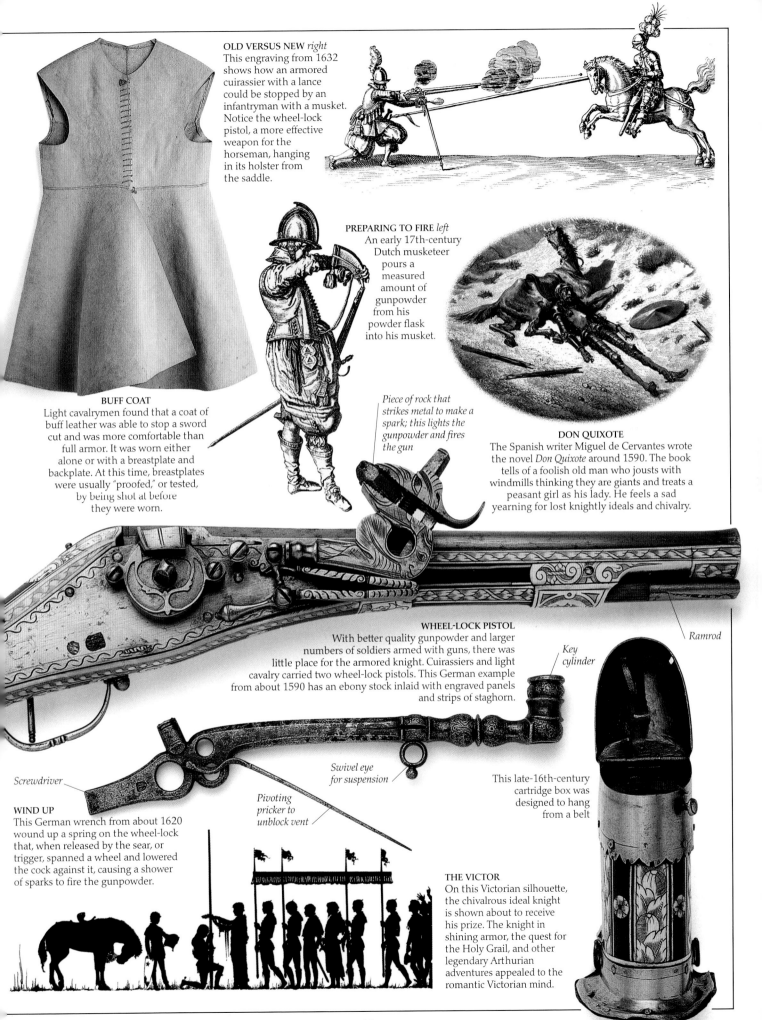

OLD VERSUS NEW *right*
This engraving from 1632 shows how an armored cuirassier with a lance could be stopped by an infantryman with a musket. Notice the wheel-lock pistol, a more effective weapon for the horseman, hanging in its holster from the saddle.

BUFF COAT
Light cavalrymen found that a coat of buff leather was able to stop a sword cut and was more comfortable than full armor. It was worn either alone or with a breastplate and backplate. At this time, breastplates were usually "proofed," or tested, by being shot at before they were worn.

PREPARING TO FIRE *left*
An early 17th-century Dutch musketeer pours a measured amount of gunpowder from his powder flask into his musket.

Piece of rock that strikes metal to make a spark; this lights the gunpowder and fires the gun

DON QUIXOTE
The Spanish writer Miguel de Cervantes wrote the novel *Don Quixote* around 1590. The book tells of a foolish old man who jousts with windmills thinking they are giants and treats a peasant girl as his lady. He feels a sad yearning for lost knightly ideals and chivalry.

Ramrod

Key cylinder

WHEEL-LOCK PISTOL
With better quality gunpowder and larger numbers of soldiers armed with guns, there was little place for the armored knight. Cuirassiers and light cavalry carried two wheel-lock pistols. This German example from about 1590 has an ebony stock inlaid with engraved panels and strips of staghorn.

Screwdriver

Swivel eye for suspension

Pivoting pricker to unblock vent

This late-16th-century cartridge box was designed to hang from a belt

WIND UP
This German wrench from about 1620 wound up a spring on the wheel-lock that, when released by the sear, or trigger, spanned a wheel and lowered the cock against it, causing a shower of sparks to fire the gunpowder.

THE VICTOR
On this Victorian silhouette, the chivalrous ideal knight is shown about to receive his prize. The knight in shining armor, the quest for the Holy Grail, and other legendary Arthurian adventures appealed to the romantic Victorian mind.

Did you know?

AMAZING FACTS

The expression "to get on your high horse" means to be overbearing or arrogant. It comes from the Middle Ages, when knights and other people of high rank rode on tall horses, called chargers. People of lower rank rode on smaller horses or ponies.

During a siege, a trebuchet was sometimes used to throw very unpleasant missiles into a castle. The severed heads of defenders, cattle dung, and dead animals that could spread disease were just some of the offerings shot over the castle walls.

Knight's tall horse known as a charger

Knight riding high on horseback

Spiral staircases were common in medieval castles. They usually spiraled in a clockwise direction. This made life difficult for an attacker fighting his way up the steep stairs, because his weapon (in his right hand) would keep hitting the post in the center of the stairs.

Samurai armor was made of iron plates laced together with silk and thread. Because the climate in Japan is damp, the armor had to be lacquered to prevent from it rusting.

The badge of the Knights Templar order was two knights riding on one horse. This represented their original state of poverty.

Krak des Chevalier

The name Templars came from the location of their headquarters, situated near the old Jewish temple in Jerusalem.

King Richard I, known as Richard the Lionheart, ruled England from 1189–1199 and was in many ways a model knight. He was a heroic fighter and zealous Crusader, and was committed to the ideal of chivalry. On his deathbed, it is said that he even pardoned the crossbowman who had fatally injured him with his arrow.

The castle of Krak des Chevaliers in Syria was a crusader castle built in the 12th century. The Knights Hospitaller lived there and defended nearby pilgrim routes against the local Muslim rulers. It had a windmill for grinding grain and its own aqueduct and nine reservoirs to supply and store water.

Just like modern tourists, medieval pilgrims wore badges on their hats to show they had been to a shrine. The badge made it clear they were on a journey and had the right to protection.

In 1212, up to 50,000 French and German children took part in a crusade to the Holy Land. Few of them ever returned home.

Castle defenders often dropped missiles onto attackers below. Hot water, red-hot sand, rocks, or quicklime were often used. But boiling oil, beloved of modern moviemakers, is rarely mentioned in contemporary chronicles.

Pivoting wooden arm

Sling pouch

Ladders used to scale the city walls

Trebuchet

The siege of Jerusalem by the Christian crusaders in 1099

QUESTIONS AND ANSWERS

Q What does chivalry mean?

A During the Middle Ages, the word chivalry was used to mean the knightly class, who were known as the Chivalry. The name comes from the French word cheval, meaning horse, because knights were soldiers who rode on horseback. Over time, chivalry came to mean the qualities expected of an ideal knight, such as courtesy, bravery, and honor.

Q Were tournaments dangerous?

A A tournament or tourney was a mock battle, designed to keep the knights fit and entertain the ladies and other members of the court, but it could be very dangerous and bloody. At one tourney held in Cologne, Germany, more than 60 knights were killed.

Q What happened to knights who were defeated in battle?

A If a knight defeated an opponent in battle, he would not necessarily kill him. An enemy knight could be more valuable alive than dead, since his family would pay ransom money to get him back. If the money was not forthcoming, the knight would have to remain in prison until it was!

Q Do knights still exist today?

A The only knights in suits of shining armor that exist today are all in museums, but the order of knighthood still remains in Britain. A knighthood—which means you are addressed as "Sir"—is given by the king or queen to a British subject for outstanding service to the country.

Scene from a medieval tournament

Q Who built the first English castle?

A It is hard to know for sure. However, when William of Normandy invaded England in 1066, his soldiers placed fortifications on the old Roman fort at Pevensey. They then went to build what looks like a motte and bailey at Hastings, in Sussex, and waited there for the arrival of King Harold and the English army. The building of this fortification is shown on the Bayeux Tapestry.

Q What were the crusades to the Holy Land?

A The crusades were a series of holy wars launched by the pope and other Christian leaders to recapture the Holy Land from Muslim control and to safeguard the pilgrimage routes. The crusades began in 1095, and ended in failure with the fall of Acre, the last Christian stronghold, in 1291.

Record Breakers

✤ **LONGEST RIDE IN ARMOR**
The longest recorded ride in armor was 208 miles (335 km) by Dick Brown. He left Edinburgh, Scotland, on June 10, 1989, and arrived in Dumfries, Scotland, four days later. Total riding time was 35 hours 25 minutes.

✤ **THE MOST KNIGHTS**
During the reign of Henry II (1154–1189), the king could call upon the services of more than 6,000 knights. Each knight pledged to serve in his army for 40 days each year without pay.

✤ **THE MOST EXPENSIVE KING**
When Richard I of England was captured by the Duke of Austria in 1192, England paid a ransom of 150,000 marks—a huge sum in those days, equivalent to many millions of dollars in today's money.

Soldiers constructing what could be the first English castle in 1066

Timeline

THE FIRST KNIGHTS were mounted warriors who fought for their lords and protected his peasants in the lawless conditions of ninth-century Europe. By the 11th century, a new social order was formed by these armored knights, and a whole tradition of knightly honor and pageantry was born. This order lasted until the 16th century, when professional armies of well-trained soldiers using pikes and guns replaced the armored knight. Knights also lived in Japan, and had an impact in many other countries too.

Knight Templar   Knight Hospitaller

• 771–814 CHARLEMAGNE EMPLOYS MOUNTED WARRIORS
Charlemagne, leader of the Franks, conquers much of present-day France, Germany, the Low Countries, and Italy, using many warrior horsemen in his army. He gives land as both reward and payment to those warriors who fight for him.

• 800 CHARLEMAGNE IS CROWNED EMPEROR
On Christmas Day 800, Charlemagne is crowned Emperor of the West by the pope in Rome. This new empire lasts for more than 1,000 years.

• 814 CHARLEMAGNE DIES
After the death of Charlemagne, his empire breaks up. Local lords and those mounted warrior knights who serve them offer protection to local people in return for labor, giving rise to the feudal system in western Europe.

Wooden spear with iron spearhead   Viking warriors

• c. 850 FIRST CASTLES BUILT
Earth and wooden castles are built in northwest France to protect the local lord from his enemies, and to defend him and the local people against Viking attacks. Castles are also built of stone.

• 911 NORMANDY FOUNDED
Charles III of France gives land to Viking invaders in an attempt to stop them from invading his country. The land is called Normandy, "land of the Northmen."

• 1000s THE NEW ORDER OF KNIGHTS
A new social order of mounted, armored knights develops in many parts of western Europe. These knights serve a local lord or duke and are in turn served by serfs or peasants. At first, they wear simple body armor made of mail.

• 1000s BECOMING A SQUIRE
Many squires are servants of a lower social class, but later the sons of noble families become squires too. In the 1000s and 1100s, young men wishing to become a knight first serve as squire or apprentice to a knight.

• 1066 NORMANS INVADE ENGLAND
Duke William of Normandy invades England and defeats King Harold at the Battle of Hastings. As king, William introduces the feudal system into England and builds many stone castles.

• 1095 THE CRUSADES BEGIN
The pope launches the first military crusade against Muslim occupation of the Holy Land. Many knights join this army. Further crusades are launched from Europe until Acre, the last Christian stronghold in the Holy Land, is captured by a Muslim army in 1291.

• 1118 KNIGHTS TEMPLAR FORMED IN JERUSALEM
Knights protecting Christian pilgrims in the Holy Land form a religious military order known as the Knights Templar.

• 1100s ADDED PROTECTION
Knights start to add more mail to their armor to protect their arms and legs.

• 1100s THE CODE OF CHIVALRY
A code of conduct, known as chivalry, is adopted by all knights. It requires them to behave in a courteous and civil way when dealing with their enemies and places special emphasis on courtly manners toward women.

Mail body armor

A Norman knight

• 1100s THE FIRST TOURNAMENTS
Tournaments, or mock battles, are first fought to train knights for battle. These events take place over large parts of the countryside.

• 1100s THE BIRTH OF HERALDRY
Decorations on shields now become more standardized using a set of rules known as heraldry. This increasingly elaborate system allows for a knight to be identified by the symbols on his shield or by his full coat-of-arms.

• 1100s NEW SIEGE MACHINES
The first trebuchets—pivoting sling catapults—are used in siege warfare in western Europe. They join existing weapons such as catapults, battering rams, and ballistas—large, mounted crossbows—in besieging and attacking castles.

• 1100s AGE OF THE TROUBADOURS
Troubadours, or minstrels, from southern France popularize poems of courtly love, romance, and chivalry. Stories about King Arthur and his Knights of the Round Table become increasingly popular throughout western Europe.

• 1185 SHOGUN JAPAN
A samurai warrior class led by the Shogun or military leader take power in Japan, although the emperor is still the official ruler of the country.

• 1189–1199 RICHARD I
Richard Coeur de Lion, nicknamed the "the Lionheart," rules England. He fights in the Third Crusade, from 1190–92, and is a prisoner from 1192–94.

• 1190 THE TEUTONIC KNIGHTS
A new religious and military order of knights—the Teutonic Knights—is formed to fight in the crusades, but soon turns its attention to converting pagans to Christianity in eastern Europe.

• 1200s ADDED HORSEPOWER
Most knights now have at least two warhorses, as well as a destrier for jousting, a sumpter or packhorse for carrying baggage, and a palfrey for long, difficult journeys.

• 1200s SAFER TOURNAMENTS
Blunted weapons are introduced at tournaments to make the contests safer. A new form of contest—jousts—is also introduced, in which two knights fight each other on horseback with lances or sometimes swords.

• 1200s THE RISING COST OF KNIGHTHOOD
The cost of becoming a knight is now so expensive that many young men avoid being knighted and remain as squires. In later years, the word squire comes to mean a gentleman who owns land.

• 1280s NEW WEAPONS
Pointed swords replace double-edged cutting swords as the main fighting weapon for knights. These are more effective, since they can be thrust between the plates of armor that knights now wear to protect themselves.

• 1300s NEW PLATED ARMOR
Knights now begin to add steel plates to their armor to protect their limbs. They also wear a coat-of-plates, made of pieces of iron riveted to a cloth covering, to protect their body even more.

• 1300s THE ARRIVAL OF CANNON
Cannon now appear on the battlefield to replace battering rams, catapults, and other manual machines in siege warfare.

• 1300s JOUSTING ON FOOT
Combat between two knights on foot becomes increasingly popular at tournaments. The contestants use swords and are allowed a set number of blows. By the 1400s, such contests have developed into more complex events involving javelins and axes as well as swords.

• 1300s DEFENSE AGAINST THE KNIGHT
In 1302, Flemish footsoldiers using clubs defeat French mounted knights at the Battle of Courtrai. Scottish spear formations using pikes stop a charge by English mounted knights and defeat them at the Battle of Bannockburn in 1314. Both battles prove that knights are not invincible.

• 1337–1453 THE HUNDRED YEARS' WAR
In 1337, Edward III of England claims the French throne and invades France. War between the two countries continues on and off for more than 100 years. Thanks to their longbowmen, the English achieve decisive victories over French knights at Crécy (1346), Poitiers (1356), and Agincourt (1415). The codes of chivalry are often ignored in this brutal war.

• 1400 FULL BODY ARMOR
Knights begin to wear full suits of plate armor, giving them allover body protection.

• 1476–1477 FRANCE vs. BURGUNDY
War between France and Burgundy shows how mounted knights are unable to defeat solid bodies of pikemen backed up by soldiers using handguns. Infantry, instead of cavalry, now become the most important members of the army.

• 1494 FRANCE INVADES ITALY
The invasion of northern Italy by France in 1494 leads to a lengthy power struggle for supremacy in Europe between France and the Hapsburg empire of Spain and Austria. Conflict between the two powers continues for most of the next century.

• 1500s DESIGNER ARMOR
Those knights still wearing armor etch designs into the metal with acid. Gold plating, or gilding, is sometimes used for added decoration.

Edward the Black Prince, English hero of the Battle of Crécy

Italian barbute or iron helmet, 1445

• 1500s A PROFESSIONAL ARMY
Paid, permanent armies of well-trained soldiers backed up by mercenaries and locally recruited men gradually replace the feudal armies of previous years. Knights now play a less effective role in battle.

• 1517 THE REFORMATION
In Germany, Martin Luther starts a revolt against the Roman Catholic Church that leads to the creation of Protestant churches throughout western Europe and more than a century of bitter religious conflict.

• 1600s THE END OF THE TOURNAMENT
During the 1600s, the tournament is replaced in most countries by displays of horsemanship called carousels.

• 1600s THE END OF AN ERA
As warfare becomes the job of full-time soldiers and mercenaries, the era of the knight comes to an end. Knighthood now becomes a title granted by the monarch to a person he or she wishes to reward.

Martin Luther preaching for a reformed church in Germany

Find out more

IF YOU ARE NOW A FAN of knights and the medieval world of castles, battles, and jousts in which they lived, here are some ways that you can find out more about them. Of course you can't go back in time to meet real knights for yourself, but you can visit some of the many castles they lived in. Your local museum may have an exhibit about knights, and perhaps even a few suits of armor, and you can also visit some of the best museums and castles—listed on page 69. Your local library and bookshop will have plenty of books for you to read about knights, and there are often programs and movies on TV and DVD for you to watch at home. Above all, check out the internet—some of the best web sites to visit are listed below—and you too will soon become a dedicated knight-watcher.

DESIGN YOUR OWN COAT-OF-ARMS
You can design your own or your family's coat-of-arms and use it to decorate your personal letters and belongings. The symbols you choose should be something special to you or have some connection to your name or to the place where you live. Read up about coats-of-arms and heraldry in books at your local library, or use the web site listed below to find out more about this fascinating subject.

Narrow slit in helmet to see through

Late 15th-century German "Gothic" style armor

The Great Hall, Warwick Castle, England

SEE ARMOR IN A MUSEUM
You can see knights' armor in various museums, castles, and stately homes in Europe and North America. One of the best collections is in the Royal Armories in Leeds, Yorkshire, England.

RETURN TO MEDIEVAL TIMES!
You can see how knights lived and fought in the dramatic reconstructions of medieval life that exist in some old castles, notably Warwick Castle, in England. Here you can see how a knight prepared for battle, as well as visit the armory and explore the medieval gatehouse, towers, and ramparts, and the magnificent Great Hall and other state rooms.

USEFUL WEBSITES

- Online home of the arms and armor department at the Metropolitan Museum of Art in New York:
  www.metmuseum.org/Works_of_Art/arms_and_armor
- Web site for kids about medieval armor and knights at the Cleveland Museum of Art:
  www.clevelandart.org/kids/armor/index.html
- A directory of Renaissance fairs around the country, with information on modern jousting troupes:
  www.faires.com
- Site of the International Jousting Association, with information on where you can see live tournaments:
  www.worldjousting.com/
- Heraldry site where you can look up the history of your family's name and coat-of-arms, with clip art section to help you create your own coat-of-arms:
  www.digiserve.com/heraldry/

VISIT A MEDIEVAL CASTLE

Visit a medieval castle and see how it was built to withstand an attack from an enemy or used to keep the local population under control. You can usually walk on the ramparts, climb the towers, and descend deep underground into the dungeons, where the prisoners were kept. Inside, you can explore the living quarters where the knights eat and slept, and see the kitchens where the food was prepared for the hungry inhabitants.

Château de Saumur in the Loire Valley, France

SEE FIGHTING AND JOUSTING

Medieval knights fighting and jousting with each other is not just a thing of the past. Some historical reenactment groups put on displays of fighting or jousting today. Look in the useful Web sites box on the opposite page for more details. If you are lucky, you could even see a full-scale reenactment of a medieval tournament.

Sir Galahad is introduced to King Arthur and the Knights of the Round Table

King Arthur

Modern day jouster charges his opponent with a lance

STORIES OF KING ARTHUR

You can read stories about knights and their daring adventures in the tales of the legendary King Arthur and his Knights of the Round Table. There is still much dispute about who King Arthur was, or whether he actually existed at all, but most people now believe that he was a British chieftain or warrior who led the resistance to the Saxon invasion of England in the fifth or sixth centuries. Many places in southern England, notably Tintagel in Cornwall, are associated with the king, and many books have been written about him.

Places to Visit

METROPOLITAN MUSEUM OF ART, NEW YORK, NEW YORK

www.metmuseum.org
This museum's collection of arms and armor consists of about 15,000 objects dating from 400 BCE to the 19th century. Western Europe and Japan are most strongly represented, but there are also items from throughout Asia and North America. Highlights include:
• the armor of King Henry II of France
• German shields from the late 15th century
• armor made in the English royal workshops at Greenwich, near London, for Tudor courtiers.

HIGGINS ARMORY MUSEUM, WORCESTER, MASSACHUSETTS

www.higgins.org
This museum is entirely dedicated to the study and display of arms and armor. Special programs explain how knights would have used weaponry in battle and tournaments.
Be sure to see:
• the complete suit of armor of Count Franz von Teuffenbach of Styria, made around 1540
• the steel gauntlets that belonged to King Philip of Spain.

ART INSTITUTE OF CHICAGO, CHICAGO, ILLINOIS

www.artic.edu
The museum's Harding Collection includes more than 1,500 artifacts of medieval life. The permanent collection contains:
• suits of armor, including an elaborate suit of Italian field armor
• weapons such as swords, daggers, and polearms.

CLEVELAND MUSEUM OF ART, CLEVELAND, OHIO

www.clevelandart.org
This museum has a medieval court featuring a full set of armor for a knight and his horse, and many other treasures.

WARWICK CASTLE, ENGLAND

A medieval castle that is also one of the finest stately homes in England. Reenactments of medieval life and jousting take place here during the summer months. The main sights include:
• the armory that features a massive 14th-century two-handed sword and a fully armored knight on horseback
• the Kingmaker Exhibition that recreates medieval life and the Wars of the Roses
• 14th-century ramparts and towers.

THE TOWER OF LONDON

This medieval fortress on the Thames River is guarded by the Yeoman Warders, popularly known as Beefeaters. Among the attractions here are:
• The White Tower, commissioned by William the Conqueror in 1078 and completed 21 years later
• The Crown Jewels, which include the crowns, scepters, and orbs used at royal coronations and other state occasions.

Glossary

BALLISTA A weapon used in siege warfare, consisting of a giant crossbow mounted on a frame that shot bolts.

BARBARIANS Uncivilized people. The word is often used to describe the many tribes who invaded the Roman Empire in the 4th and 5th centuries CE.

BATTLEMENT The top part of a castle wall that had gaps in it through which archers could shoot at attackers.

BIT The metal part of a bridle that fits inside the horse's mouth and is used to control the horse.

BODKIN A long, thin arrowhead, shaped like a needle.

BOLT An arrow to be shot from a weapon such as a crossbow or ballista.

BUTT A target set on a mound of earth, used by archers for shooting practice.

CATAPULT An engine for throwing missiles.

CHALICE A cup used to hold the wine in the Christian service of Mass, or the Holy Communion.

CHIVALRY Originally meaning horsemanship, chivalry came to refer to the combination of qualities expected of an ideal knight, such as courage, honor, and courtesy. In the 12th century, this behavior was extended to form a knightly code of conduct, with a special emphasis on courtly manners toward women.

COAT-OF-ARMS A set of symbols used by a knight on his shield or surcoat to identify him in battle or at a tournament.

Bodkin

COAT-OF-PLATES A form of body armor invented in the 14th century, consisting of a number of pieces of iron riveted to a cloth covering.

CRENEL A gap on the top part of a castle wall through which defenders could shoot at attackers.

CROSSBOW A bow fixed across a wooden handle with a groove for a bolt. Various mechanisms were developed to help pull back the cord. The cord was then released to shoot the bolt.

CRUSADES A series of military expeditions made by European knights during the Middle Ages. The goal of the crusades was to capture the Holy Land from Muslim control.

DESTRIER A knight's warhorse.

DUBBING The ceremony at which a squire was made a knight. The king or another knight tapped the squire on the neck with a sword, then the new knight was presented with his sword and spurs.

EFFIGY A sculpture of a person. In the Middle Ages, many wealthy people's tombs were decorated with a life-size effigy of them.

EMBRASURE An alcove set in a castle wall with a small opening through which archers, crossbowmen, or gunners could shoot.

ETCHING Using acid to "eat" a design on exposed parts of metal. Suits of armor were sometimes etched with patterns.

FEUDAL SYSTEM A social system used in Europe during the Middle Ages, under which a local lord gave land to his vassals in return for their allegiance and service.

GARRISON A group of soldiers stationed in a castle or town to defend it.

GATEHOUSE The entrance to a castle. The gatehouse was often protected with heavily fortified towers, a portcullis, drawbridge, and a ditch or moat outside.

GILDING Putting a thin covering of gold on an object to decorate it.

HERALDRY A system of using symbols on knights' shields or coats-of-arms, so that they could be easily identified in battle or in tournaments.

HERETIC Someone whose religious views are unacceptable to the mainstream church.

HOLY GRAIL According to legend, the Holy Grail was the cup that Jesus used at the Last Supper. In the stories of King Arthur, many of his knights went on quests to find the Holy Grail.

INFANTRY Soldiers who fought on foot.

JOUST A combat between two mounted knights armed with lances. Jousting was invented to allow knights to show off their battle skills.

Gatehouse to Caerphilly Castle, Wales

KEEP A strong stone tower that formed part of a castle. They were probably used for storage, or as living quarters.

KNIGHT A warrior who fought on horseback. The term is normally used for the period c. 800–1600, when warriors fought with swords and lances instead of guns and other small arms.

KNIGHTS HOSPITALLER A military order of monks who also cared for the sick. They were also known as the Knights of St. John.

KNIGHTS TEMPLAR An order of monks who were also fighting knights. They fought against the Muslims and protected Christian pilgrims in the Holy Land.

LANCE A long weapon with a wooden shaft and a pointed metal head. Knights used lances when charging on horseback.

LONGBOW A large bow used during the Middle Ages. It was usually made of yew wood and could shoot arrows up to 1,100 ft (300 m) away.

Embrasure in a castle wall

Joust at Tours in France, 1446

LUGS Two small cross-pieces on a spear or sword that prevented the weapon from being pushed too far into an opponent's body and getting stuck.

MACE A heavy weapon, consisting of a metal head on top of a wooden pole.

MAIL A form of armor made up of many small linked iron rings. Mail could be made into garments, such as coats or mittens.

MERCENARY A hired soldier who fought simply for money.

MOOR A Muslim from northwest Africa.

MOTTE AND BAILEY An early style of castle. The motte was a mound with a wooden tower on top; the bailey was a courtyard below the motte that contained the domestic buildings. The bailey was surrounded by a wooden fence and a ditch to keep out intruders.

NORMANS People who came from Normandy in northern France. The Normans were descended from the Vikings who settled in the region during the 10th century. The Normans conquered England under their leader, Duke William of Normandy, in 1066.

PAGE A young boy servant in the household of a king or great knight. Pages were usually the sons of noble families and were in training to become knights when they were older.

Model of a Japanese samurai

Reenactment of Japanese feudal lords paying their respects to the Shogun

PALFREY A horse used for long journeys.

PEASANT A farm laborer or other person who works for a lord.

PILGRIMAGE A journey to a sacred place for religious reasons. In the Middle Ages, some Christians went on pilgrimages to Jerusalem and other sites in the Holy Land, and to the tombs of famous saints, such as that of St. Peter in Rome.

PLATE ARMOR Body armor made of large metal pieces, as opposed to mail.

POMMEL A round knob on the end of a sword handle that helped to balance the weight of the blade.

PORTCULLIS A metal gate, or an iron-clad wooden gate, that could be lowered in front of the entrance to a castle to stop attackers getting in.

QUIVER A bag hung from an archer's back, or more usually his waist, in which he stored his arrows.

RANSOM A sum of money demanded for the release of a prisoner, such as a lord or knight, who was captured or defeated in battle. The captors demanded the ransom from the prisoner's family.

SAMURAI A Japanese warrior.

SARACEN A name used at the time of the Crusades for all Muslims and Arabs. The Saracens were originally nomadic people who lived in the Syrian and Arabian deserts.

SCALING LADDER A long ladder used by attacking soldiers to try to climb over the wall of a castle.

SCONCE A candlestick for hanging on a wall.

SERF A laborer who was not allowed to leave the land on which he worked.

SHOGUN A Japanese military leader.

SHRINE A holy site, such as a saint's tomb.

SPUR A V-shaped device, with a spiked wheel, that a knight fitted to the inside of his heels and used to urge his horse forward.

SQUIRE A young man who served as an attendant to a knight. A squire was usually the son of a noble family and was himself in training to become a knight.

Spur

STIRRUPS Two loops suspended from a horse's saddle to support the rider's feet.

SURCOAT A loose coat or robe worn over armor. A knight's surcoat was sometimes decorated with his coat-of-arms.

TILT A barrier used in jousting to separate two charging knights and avoid collisions.

TOURNAMENT A pageant that included mock battles, jousting, and foot combat, in which knights practiced their fighting skills, often using blunted weapons.

TREBUCHET A weapon used in siege warfare to throw large missiles at a castle.

TROUBADOURS Medieval French poets who composed and sang poems on the theme of courtly love.

VISOR The moveable part of a helmet that covered the face.

WINDLASS A machine with a horizontal axle, used to wind back catapults and ballistas, as well as some later powerful crossbows.

Index

Acknowledgments

Dorling Kindersley would like to thank:
The Wallace Collection, the Royal Armories, the British Museum, & the Museum of the Order of St. John, for provision of objects for photography; English Heritage, the National Trust, & Cadw (Welsh Historical Monuments), for permission to photograph at Rochester, Bodiam, & Caerphilly castles; David Edge for information on items in the Wallace Collection; Paul Cannings, Jonathan Waller, John Waller, Bob Dow, Ray Monery, & Julia Harris for acting as models; Anita Burger for makeup; Joanna Cameron for illustrations (pages 22–23); Angels & Burmans for costumes.

For this edition, the publisher would also like to thank: the author for assisting with revisions; Claire Bowers, David Ekholm-JAlbum, Sunita Gahir, Joanne Little, Nigel Ritchie, Susan St. Louis, Carey Scott, & Bulent Yusuf for the clip art; David Ball, Neville Graham, Rose Horridge, Joanne Little, & Sue Nicholson for the wall chart.; BCP, Marianne Petrou, & Owen Peyton Jones for checking the digitized files.

The publisher would like to thank the following for their kind permission to reproduce their images:

Picture credits t=top, b=bottom, c=center, l=left, r= right

Ancient Art & Architecture Collection: 58cl, 58c, 58tr, 59bl, 65b.
Board of the Trustees of the Armories: 70tl.
Bridgeman Art Library, London/New York: 53b/Biblioteca Estense, Modena; 10b/Bibliotheque de L'Arsenal, Paris: 64br/British Library: 19tc, 20tr, 20c, 38cr, 39c, 49tr, 54tl//Bibliotheque Municipal de Lyon: 55c/Bibliotheque Nationale, Paris: 11br, 15tr, 22cr, 25tl, 41tr, 42bl, 43t, 54bl, 57tr/Corpus Christi College, Cambridge: 13rc/Corpus Christi College, Oxford: 54br/Musee Conde, Chantilly: 50bl, 51bl, 65t/ Vatican Library, Rome: 50br// Victoria & Albert Museum: 37cl/Wrangham Collection: 59c.
British Museum: 71cr.
Burgerbibliothek, Bern: 25rc.

Christ Church, Oxford/Photo: Bodleian Library: 27tl.
Dorling Kindersley: Photo from *Children just Like Me* by Barnabus & Anabel Kindersley, published by DK: 71bl.
E.T. Archive: 6bl, 11tl, 18bl, 27tr, 30bl, 31bl, 33cl, 33cr, 39tr, 41c, 49bl, 57bc, 58rc, 59cl, 60c/British Library: 19bc, 32c/ British Museum: 27bl/ Fitzwilliam Museum, Cambridge: 48rc.
Mary Evans Picture Library: 69bl.
Robert Harding Picture Library: 8tl, 12rc, 18tr, 22bl, 26c, 34br, 34bl, 55bl/British Library: 11c, 34cl, 44b, 45bl.
Heritage Images: British Library 46bl.
Michael Holford: 8bl, 9tr, 52c, 55br.
Hulton-Deutsch Collection: 56cl.
A.F. Kersting: 9cl.
Mansell Collection: 11bl, 21c, 39tr, 46br, 55tl, 63bl/Alinari: 46tr.
Bildarchiv Foto Marburg: 48br.
Arxiu Mas: 54cl.
Stadtbibliothek Nurnberg: 17rc.
Osterreichische Nationalbibliotehek, Vienna (Cod.2597, f.15): 40br.

Pierpont Morgan Library, New York: 29c.
Scala: 7br, 33t, 34tlc, 36cl.
Stiftsbibliothek St Gallen: 6c.
Syndication International: 26br, 27cl, 27tcl, 32bc, 37tl, 41tl, 50tr, 53l, 57tl/Photo Trevor Wood: 36tr.
Warwick Castle: 68cb.

Wall chart: DK Images: Judith Miller / Otford Antiques and Collectors Center 1bl (Brooch); Judith Miller / Sloan's 1tr; Michael Holford: 1clb (Pilgrimage)

Jacket: *Front:* Jonathan Blair/Corbis, b; Archivo Iconografico, S.A./Corbis, tl; Wallace Collection, London, UK, tcl, tcr. *Back:* British Museum, crb; Royal Armouries, Board of Trustees of the Armouries, br; Wallace Collection, bl, ca, l.

All other images © Dorling Kindersley.
For further information see:
www.dkimages.com